THE ULTIMATE TAX STRATEGY GUIDE

Powerful Techniques to Lower Personal Taxes Tremendously and Build Tax-Free Wealth for Retirement

ANDREW DIXON

Table of Contents

Section 1: Introduction to Taxes 1

    Chapter 1: All income is not equal: how tax law favors the wealthy 5

    Chapter 2: Deductions and Credits 21

Section 2: Maximizing accrual: work now, play later 29

    Chapter 3: Retirement income 31

Section 3: On your own 50

    Chapter 4: Individual Retirement Accounts (IRAs) 50

    Chapter 5: Social Security 63

Section 4: Accumulating Wealth 73

    Chapter 6: Investing in stocks 74

Section 5: Real Estate 96

    Chapter 7: Residential Real Estate 100

    Chapter 8: Multi-family housing and commercial property 110

    Chapter 9: Fractional investments 116

Section 6: Maximizing Accumulation 120

    Chapter 10: Deferring taxes on capital gains 122

    Chapter 11: Minimizing Capital Gains on Stocks 134

    Chapter 12: Estate Planning 139

Section 1

Introduction to Taxes

Rob Knauerhase, an obscure but clever pundit, declared, "Isn't it appropriate that the month of the tax begins with April Fool's Day and ends with cries of 'May Day!'?"

Many of us share this sentiment when slogging through the annual April chore of tax preparation and payment. Few of us understand it, and most of us dread it. Those who claim a yearly refund from the IRS declare themselves winners of the game. In fact, those taxpayers have just been repaid for an interest-free loan they voluntarily made to the federal government by having more than necessary withheld from their paychecks. The goal should be to come out even, certainly to lower the overall obligation, but to do so in a way that allows us to retain use of our funds, not pay them and then wait to have them returned.

Ordinary income, what most of us earn in salary or hourly wages, is taxed at a progressive rate of up to 37 percent. What does progressive mean? It means that the higher your ordinary income rises, the higher percentage you pay on the amount. It's almost a penalty for earning more. In this way, income taxes appear on the surface to place a heavier burden on those with higher incomes. After all, if you earn $40,000 as a single filer, your federal tax obligation is 12%. If you make over $518,400 as a single filer, the rate is 37%.

Remember when Warren Buffet reported that he paid a lower tax rate than his secretary, thanks to the loopholes and deductions available to him but not to her? It was a true statement for him personally, although perhaps not widely true at the time. **Today the wealthiest individuals, as a group, pay a lower total tax percentage than any other group of citizens**.

The dynamic has been shifting over time, and the elite echelon of the 400 highest earners in the U.S. crossed over as a group in 2019 to enjoy paying a lower percentage of their income than every other identified population segment. That total was 23% (down from 47% in 1980 and 70% in 1950, according to the *New York Times*).

Other types of earnings, such as profit from a business or gains on a capital investment, are taxed differently, and sometimes not at all. If you increase what you earn from these other types of income, the percentage of the tax does not increase. This fact is one reason why tax law is said to favor the wealthy. In simple terms, it does.

Some of the income that the "one percent" earns isn't considered taxable income by the Internal Revenue Service. As a result, it may not need to be reported. Examples of income that do not need to be reported by the recipient include gifts, inheritances (although in some cases the giver or the estate will need to declare the gift or taxable bequest), and alimony (related to marriages dissolved during or after 2019).

If the income is reportable and taxable, the taxpayer may be able to decide when the taxable event takes place, and the timing may influence the taxable status. Recognition of capital gains are an excellent example of this category, and we will discuss these in greater detail later.

To give you one example, suppose you have a bad year and lose money in the stock market; you earn less income for that year. The losses you incur can be balanced against other income, reducing your overall income. Suppose your capital losses exceed any capital gains you made in other areas. You can offset ordinary taxable income with those losses, up to $3,000 in any tax year.

If the net capital losses exceed $3,000, you can hold onto (carry forward) the excess and use it to continue offsetting either capital losses or ordinary income in future years until the total loss has been used up.

However, any of us can use these facts to our advantage if we know how. This guide will explain the differences between income types and describe how you can use the same tax minimization methods and wealth accumulation successful investors enjoy.

In the first section, we will explore tax law, the different ways income is taxed, and how this favors those already wealthy.

Chapter 1

All income is not equal:

how tax law favors the wealthy

Capital gains versus ordinary income

As mentioned, **ordinary income** is what we receive as a wage or salary. This money is paid to an individual for work performed. Usually, an employer pays it regularly and reports it to the federal, state, and local taxing agencies based on the taxpayer's identified reporting status. What does that mean?

When you start a new job, you fill out a form called a W-4. It is officially the Employee's Withholding Certificate, and it tells your employer what your tax filing status is. You indicate on the form whether you file your taxes as single or married, filing jointly, or head of household, etc. You also indicate the number of dependents you will be claiming on your next income tax return. The form comes with instructions and worksheets to help you determine the appropriate number to claim.

If you follow the instructions, the number of exemptions you claim should result in roughly the correct amount of federal income tax being withheld from your paychecks. When you file your tax return, you will see a small refund, small underpayment, or perfect match.

However, many things can affect the accuracy of the W-4 and create a disparity. If you have more than one job or your spouse does, there is a higher incidence of variation. People also like to "game the system" by claiming more or fewer exemptions than called for to either increase their current net pay or force savings by having more withheld than necessary.

At the end of the year (legally, before January 31 of the following tax year), the employer sends the employee a W-2 form, which shows the income and all deductions, including income taxes, Medicare and Social Security (sometimes called payroll taxes), any retirement contributions, and state and local deductions.

All that said, the lesson is that you cannot draw conclusions about a taxpayer's tax obligations by knowing whether that person receives a refund. They may be paying too much, too little, or just enough but choosing to do it on a different schedule than someone who pays precisely what is needed throughout the year and receives no refund check.

Suppose, like many people today, you work as a contractor. In that case, you will receive your earnings information in a slightly different manner, usually through the issuance of 1099 forms. The worker completes a W-9 to provide their information to the company or individual for whom they are completing work.

However, while the document does ask for a Social Security Number or Employer ID Number, it does not request tax status, because 1099 workers do not have taxes withheld. The entity paying for the work sends information about money paid on a 1099-MISC, but the worker is responsible for paying the taxes due. More about this later.

Income tax rates favor passive income.

What does that mean? It means that the income we gain through working is taxed at a higher rate than the remuneration we gain through investing (or inheriting, which is even less active than investing). Let's take a look.

Tax rates for ordinary income in 2021 range from a low of 10% for earnings under $9,950 for a single individual or $19,900 for a married couple filing jointly up to 37% for a single taxpayer with income over $523,600 ($628,300 for a married couple filing jointly). Right in the middle of the middle class (or even toward the lower end of the middle class in a high-cost state), if you are a single person with an income of $86,375, your tax rate is 24%. A married couple with an income of $81,050 filing jointly is subject to a tax rate of 22%.

Remember, we defined ordinary income as the pay we get for working. It actually includes a bit more than just that. The IRS defines ordinary income as all the following:

hourly wages, salaries, tips, commissions, interest earned from bonds, income earned from a business, some rents and royalties, short-term capital gains held for no more than a year, and unqualified dividends.

We will break this down, because the distinctions are crucial to your understanding of how to ascertain income on which you can avoid and defer taxes.

Let's start with capital gains. What are they, and what is the difference between short-term and long-term?

Simply put, a capital gain is a profit from the sale of a property or an investment. If you buy a piece of property for $100 and sell it for $200, the capital gain is $100. If you purchase a stock share for $10 and sell it for $20, the capital gain is $10. Those are the most common examples, but almost anything can be included, like wine, baseball memorabilia, antiques, art, vintage automobiles, and so on.

A **short-term capital gain** is a profit obtained in the sale of an asset you have held for one year or less. A **long-term capital gain** is a profit obtained by the sale of an asset held for longer than one year. The determination of profit or loss is the price of the sale minus the **basis**. The basis is usually the amount you paid for the asset but not always.

We will discuss adjustments to basis in greater detail later when we dig into real estate and inheritances. Both of these situations have implications to the cost basis that are important.

Suppose you buy a stock for $200 and sell it for $300, but you only held onto it for six months. That $100 profit is a short-term capital gain, and you will report it as ordinary income, paying taxes on it equal to the tax rate for your regular pay. Instead, suppose you buy that stock for $200, hold it for 367 days, and sell it for $300. The $100 profit is now a long-term capital gain. What's the tax rate now?

The answer depends on your tax rate overall. Still, it will definitely be less than the percentage you would pay for ordinary income. For a married couple filing jointly, if your taxable income is less than $80,800, your tax rate on a long-term capital gain is 0%. That's right, nothing.

To revisit the situation mentioned previously in which the single individual is paying a 24% tax rate and the married couple is paying a 22% tax rate on ordinary income (wages), both of these illustrative taxpayers would be responsible for paying a long-term capital gains assessment rate of 15%. This scenario means that their higher income would result in some taxes being due on the capital gain but less than what they pay on the income they receive from wages or a short-term appreciation.

Dividend Income

When you invest in equities (stock), you may focus on the value (price) of the stock increasing so that you can sell the stock and enjoy the gains. We will discuss stock investments in-depth later. While you are watching the stock's value rise, you may also benefit from dividends paid by the corporation that issued the stock.

What is a dividend? In simple terms, payment of dividends is how the corporation shares its profits with the shareholders. If you own 100 shares in ABC Company, and that company issues a dividend of $2 per share, you will receive $200. It is essential to note that in order to receive the dividend payment, you must have purchased the stock by the **ex-dividend date**, which is the date before the date of record. If you sell the shares after the ex-dividend date, you would still be eligible to collect the dividend (if you purchased them before). The date of record is the date of the dividend declaration.

Not all companies issue dividends, and those that do distribute them on a schedule their board of directors approves. Many well-known U.S. corporations pay dividends regularly, and some investors rely on the income these payments provide. Some of the numerous companies that traditionally pay dividends include Apple, Disney, Target, and Exxon. There is an elite group of dividend payors called Dividend Aristocrats. This list of companies is notable for paying out and increasing the dividend each distributes every year for at least 25 years. The list is topped by Genuine Parts (which trades under GPC) and Dover Corp (DOV), which have maintained and increased their dividend payouts for 65 and 64 years, respectively. Others holding lofty positions on the list are Proctor & Gamble (PG), 3M (MMM), Coca-Cola (KO), and Johnson & Johnson (JNJ). From time to time, a trusted dividend-paying company drops off the list for various reasons, usually accompanied by an outcry from the shareholders.

When we dig deep into stock investing later in the book, we will cover mutual funds in detail. However, it is relevant to the topic of dividends and dividend taxes to note that specific mutual funds also pay dividends, and you can buy these designated funds without having to identify and purchase individual equities. The niche market is called dividend exchange-traded funds, and there are many from which to choose. They may have a broad market diversity or specialize in a particular sector. Still, they contain stocks that pay regular dividends. Like other exchange-traded funds (but unlike mutual funds, which trade after the market closes each day), these trade throughout the day.

Taxing Dividends

Like capital gains, dividend income may be taxed either at the higher rate associated with ordinary income or lower capital. Remember, the standard income rate starts at 10% and goes up to 37%, while the assessment on a capital gain begins at 0 and tops out at 20%. For your qualified dividend income exposed to that 20% rate, your income level would need to be relatively high. Most taxpayers will not find their qualified dividends (or long-term capital gains) taxed at a rate higher than 15%.

What is a qualified dividend?

A qualified dividend is paid from ownership of a share in a domestic company (and certain foreign corporations), which the investor has held for a specific time, referred to as the **holding period**. During that time, you must not have **hedged** your position. Usually, for common stock, the eligibility requirement is that the investor has held the stock for more than 60 days of the 121 days, starting 60 days before the ex-dividend date (which is one day before the date of record).

What is hedging?

Hedging is like buying insurance. You may have heard the expression "hedging your bets," which means accepting less upside in return for less potential downside. The same is true of hedging with stocks. You hedge a trade in one way by offsetting the investment in another. Some typical hedging strategies include options and futures, which are types of derivatives.

An option is a contract that gives the investor the ability to purchase or sell a stock at a specific price, either for a period of time or at a date in the future. The right to buy the stock is a "call option," and the right to sell for a certain price is a "put option." The future price is referred to as the exercise price or strike price. These options are sometimes granted to employees as a method of profit sharing or incentive, but they are also ways to hedge a position in a particular holding.

If you are "bullish" about the prospects of a stock (or a fund or index), you can leverage your available funds and limit the risk by buying call options. You think the price will go up, but you aren't sure enough or don't have enough money to risk by going all in on buying shares, so you buy the options.

If you are a "bear" on a stock, you buy the "put option" which will increase in value if the stock you have targeted loses value as expected. This is less risky than going short on the stock, because you aren't in danger of losing money if the stock price increases instead; you just let the option expire.

Reporting dividend income

Earlier, we talked about the IRS Form 1099 for income paid to contractors. There is another version of the 1099, the 1099-DIV, on which dividend income is reported. Box 1a will include distributions made as ordinary dividends, taxable as such, while Box 1b shows qualified dividends.

One more thing about capital gains and dividends: net investment income tax

The Health Care and Reconciliation Act of 2010 (the final version of the Affordable Care Act) included the so-called Medicare surtax, formally called a net investment income tax (NIIT). This charge is a 3.8% tax that some individuals and trusts must pay in certain circumstances. You will pay the surtax if your MAGI (modified adjusted gross income) and your net investment income exceed specific amounts. Form 8690 can help you figure it out, but here are some general guides:

MAGI is your AGI (adjusted gross income) plus things you deducted to find the AGI (like IRA contributions, student loan interest, any taxable Social Security income, and passive losses). If your MAGI is higher than the amount the IRS has set as the threshold for your filing status, you need to pay the NIIT.

Your net investment income includes interest, capital gains and dividends, rent and royalties, earnings from passive investing, and non-qualified annuity distributions. It excludes wages, unemployment payments, income from self-employment and Social Security, and distributions from qualified retirement plans. But you can deduct the expenses associated with that investment income. Deductible expenses include broker fees, local and state income taxes paid, the cost of tax preparation and investment advice, and the costs associated with the rental or royalty income.

You can see that the calculation isn't simple, and a tax advisor's support is warranted. To add to the complexity, the amount of income on which the 3.8% is due can either be the amount of the net investment income (NII) if that is lower than the amount by which your MAGI exceeds the IRS limit, or the difference between the two if that figure is less.

Business Income

As renowned investor Warren Buffet famously said, "If you think being an entrepreneur is risky, try working for someone else for 40 years and living off Social Security."

Many people think the key to wealth accumulation is building a business. It is important to note that Buffet also believes, "If you don't find a way to make money while you sleep, you will work until you die."

Starting a business (whether involving active work, passive income accumulation, or both) is doubtless a critical method of increasing income. Later in this guide, we will investigate some investment options like stocks and real estate that do, indeed, make money for you while you are sleeping (or doing most anything else). In this section we will look at the tax advantages of business income versus ordinary income.

Pass-through business tax deduction

The 2017 Tax Cut and Jobs Act (TCJA) included a provision that was touted as providing needed assistance to small businesses, establishing a tax deduction for owners of pass-through businesses, which is less formally known as "the 20% deduction." A pass-through business means that the company itself does not pay corporate taxes; it "passes through" the business's income to the owner, who then pays the taxes on a personal return at an individual rate. If the company makes a profit, that is income; if the business has a loss, that is a deduction from other ordinary income the owner earns.

The pass-through business could be a sole proprietorship, an S corporation, a partnership (regular or limited liability), or an LLC. It cannot be a C corporation, a legally structured company in which the business pays taxes on profits. However, the TCJA established a permanent 21% tax rate for C corporations, as well.

While the new 20% deduction was advertised as help for small businesses (and it was welcomed by all business owners), it is primarily bolstering the wealthy. Here's why:

Most pass-through income (remember, that's income from a business which is paid on the owner's tax return) is passing through to the "one percent." Over half of pass-through income flows to that group, which derives a full fifth of their income from pass-throughs. Compare that to the bottom 67% of earners, who shared a mere 4% of pass-through money.

What does this mean? At the beginning of this discussion we noted that the wealthy are getting their income from sources that make it easier for them to pay lower taxes than the non-wealthy. The top 1% of earners get 20% of their income from business income rather than from wages, salaries, commissions, and the other types of ordinary income that is taxed at the higher rate.

That top 1% of earners are getting a full 50% of income from those businesses which have the favorable tax treatment, while the other 99% of us are sharing the other half.

The benefit to the higher income taxpayer is enhanced because the deduction is worth more to them. If you are in the top tax bracket with a 37% tax rate, each dollar of pass-through income deducted saves you 37 cents. Compare that to a middle-class earner in the 22% bracket for whom the savings is 22 cents on the dollar.

Nonetheless, for a business owner, the new provision is a boon. It allows the individual to deduct up to 20% of their qualified business income (QBI) from every pass-through business they own all or part of. The pass-through business income deduction is available to you whether you itemize your deductions or take the standard deductions, which we will discuss in more detail below. However, it does not reduce your adjusted gross income; so, it does not lower your Social Security or Medicare taxes.

Importantly, QBI does include rental income as well as income from REITs (real estate investment trusts). What it does not include are the following:

⟩ Short- or long-term capital gains
⟩ Salary or wages paid to S corporation shareholders and guaranteed payments to partners
⟩ Dividend or interest income
⟩ Most income earned outside the U.S.

Calculating the deduction depends on your total income

It gets a little complicated here (no one ever said doing your taxes would be fun). If your total income (from all sources, not just the pass-through from the business) is under the threshold set by the IRS, it stays reasonably simple. That threshold for 2021 is $164,900 for taxpayers filing with single status and $329,800 if you are married filing jointly.

If your income is under that, you can deduct the 20% of Qualified Business Income, as noted above.

Interestingly, if your income is higher than the applicable limit, your eligibility for the deduction depends to some extent on what kind of business you are operating. The instructions for the QBI computation establish a category called "specified service trade or business" which is subject to a phase-in threshold range. The following fields of endeavor are included in the SSTB (specified service trade or business) carve-out, and subject to the modified rules:

- Health care
- Law
- Accounting and actuary
- Performing arts
- Consulting
- Athletics/sports
- Financial services/brokerage (not including real estate)
- Investing and investment management
- Securities trading and dealing

> Commodities
> Partnership management
> Any trade in which the principal asset of the business is the skill or reputation of one or more of the owners or employees.

If your business falls in these categories, your deduction is limited above the threshold more than if your income is derived from another source. The analysis may leave you baffled; so, get a useful calculator or accountant if you are trying to do it yourself.

Specifically, the amount you can deduct is calculated by how much you paid out in wages to employees (including to yourself) and the value of any property your business owns. The ability to use the deduction phases out faster for business income stemming from the specified trades and businesses than from other types of small companies (remember, C corporations can't use it.)

Also, remember that even though the QBI can be up to 20% of the business's income, it can't be more than 20% of your total income. You are probably going to need professional help for this one.

Overall thoughts on taxes and how to approach them

Humorist Dave Barry always got a chuckle with this line:

"It's income tax time again, Americans: time to gather up those receipts, get out those tax forms, sharpen up that pencil, and stab yourself in the aorta."

Of course, it isn't funny; we think we are taking the steps we need to minimize our tax exposure, and then Congress passes a "reform" bill. The Tax Cuts and Jobs Act of 2017 was the most significant change to the U.S. tax code in nearly 30 years. The law did lower tax rates for corporations and the highest earners and made substantial changes to tax credits and deductions, some of which we have already reviewed. For 2020 and 2021, the standard deductions are increasing again. Here is the list of standard deduction amounts for 2020 taxes (to be filed in 2021):

- $12,400 for single taxpayers
- $12,400 for married taxpayers filing separately
- $18,650 for heads of households
- $24,800 for married taxpayers filing jointly
- $24,800 for qualifying widow(er)s

That increase, combined with limits and changes to some popular itemized deductions, has resulted in a tremendous decrease in the number of taxpayers itemizing. The TCJA capped the amount of state and local taxes (known as SALT) a household could deduct at $10,000. That was less than half of the average previously claimed by itemizers in high property tax and income tax states like California and New York. Over 44 million households claimed the SALT deduction in 2017, compared to only 16 million in 2018.

Chapter 2

Deductions and Credits

Overall, the percentage of taxpayers choosing to itemize dropped from around 30% to 10%. Many taxpayers run the numbers both ways—using the itemized approach and then comparing it to the new, higher standard deductions. There are some deductions and credits you may be overlooking. With one exception, these deductions are only available if you itemize rather than taking the standard deduction, but the credits are available regardless. Let's start with deductions and then look at credits, since those are available regardless of which deduction strategy you employ.

Itemized Deductions: changes and opportunities

I. **SALT (State and Local Taxes).** As previously discussed, this formerly high-impact deduction for many has lost some of its wallop with the passage of the TCJA. In high-tax states, the combination of state income tax and property taxes can be tremendous, even for middle-class taxpayers. The average deduction for itemizers before the TCJA was well over $20,000, but the combined deduction for the category is now $10,000. For taxpayers with most of their deduction eggs in this basket, the standard deduction option became more attractive.

II. **Mortgage Interest.** Another cherished deduction is for mortgage interest, which is still allowed for both first and second homes, but with lower limits. Interest can be deducted on a mortgage amount up to $750,000 (down from the previous limit of $1 million) but can no longer be deducted for a home equity loan unless that loan is used for improvements to the residence.

III. **Medical expenses.** The TCJA reduced the threshold for deducting medical costs (not reimbursed) from 10% to 7.5% of adjusted gross income, but it is set to return to 10% for the 2020 tax year unless Congress takes action to extend the reduction. This deduction is uncommon.

IV. **Charitable contributions.**

V. **Cash.** Charitable contributions are still deductible, and the limit was increased from 50% to 60% of adjusted gross income. However, for many taxpayers the amount they donate to nonprofits is not enough to make the difference between itemizing and taking the standard deduction. This was viewed as deleterious to the financial condition of many charitable organizations. The CARES (Coronavirus Aid, Relief and Economic Security Act) allows taxpayers to claim a deduction of up to $300 for charitable contributions made in 2020 even if they take the standard deduction.

VI. Noncash. Most of us keep track of the financial donations we give to medical research organizations, the local animal shelter, our alma mater, and other nonprofits. If you itemize, it's easy to plug these amounts into the tax return. However, keeping track of some smaller, indirect gifts can add to the total.

VII. Many parents provide materials for their child's school programs. If you make cookies or donate plants and mulch for the playground, those expenses are deductible. If you buy envelopes and stamps for a pen pal program for a nonprofit, those are, also. Keep track of the miles you drive in your car to pick up the supplies (and to deliver the children to the events), because the mileage is also reportable.

VIII. Don't forget about the clothing, books, household items, and furniture you drop off at the local thrift shop. That is a tax-deductible gift. If the value exceeds $250, you need a letter from the organization that acknowledges your assistance in addition to the receipt.

IX. **The home office deduction.** This popular and misunderstood deduction deserves its own section. The key takeaway this year is that the home office deduction is not available to employees of companies who work from home as opposed to entrepreneurs and contractors. If you filled out a W-2, you probably can't use this deduction. This news may come as a surprise, since many people have been setting up, furnishing, and running their home empires, paying extra for electricity, and surviving without an information technology help desk. But you must be self-employed or running a business to qualify for this one.

X. If you do qualify (use IRS Publication 587 for help), it can be a nice deduction. First, calculate the percentage of your home you use for the home office or running the business. The IRS says the portion must be used "exclusively and regularly" for your business activities. Let's say your home office takes up 10% of the square footage of your home. Add up the mortgage or rent, utilities, insurance, taxes, repairs, and other costs that cover the entire dwelling, and you can deduct 10% of the total.

XI. There is also a simplified version. The IRS authorizes a deduction of $5 per square foot of the home used for the business (up to 300 square feet) without the record-keeping and calculations.

XII. There are two essential things to remember. The first is the "regular and exclusive" condition. If your office is also the guest room or the music room, it doesn't qualify. The second is that it must be your primary office. It's okay if you meet clients in a public place as long as you are using the office for activities like billing, keeping records, maintaining material, etc.

XIII. **Is the home office deduction a red flag for an audit?** This rumor is either an urban myth or a well-hidden secret. The IRS doesn't disclose the reasons why they choose tax returns for audit. Still, they do report the percentages of returns audited. The overall chance of being audited stands at about 0.6 percent. For taxpayers with adjusted gross income under $1 million, it is even lower.

XIV. Some return anomalies are known to bump up the chance of an audit. The reported list includes these:

⟩ Large deductions relative to income. If you report an income of $50,000 and $40,000 in deductions, that may attract more scrutiny than a lower amount.

⟩ Casualty losses and bad debt deductions may invite attention.

⟩ Recurring business losses draw suspicion, particularly if they are routinely high.

⟩ Business deductions that don't seem applicable to the industry may increase the chance of an audit.

Tax credits: better than deductions

I. Deductions are subtracted from income, while credits are subtracted from tax owed. That's why credits are better. Suppose you have income of $100,000, and you are paying a 25% rate of income tax. If you have a deduction of $100, you reduce the overall income by $100, and you pay taxes on $99,900. With that 25% tax rate, you saved $25. But if you have a tax credit for $100, that reduces the actual tax bill by $100. Let's take a look at a few worthy credits.

II. **Child Tax Credit.** In addition to increasing the standard deduction for individuals (but eliminating the personal exemption), the TCJA temporarily doubled the maximum child tax credit for children under 17 to $2,000 per child. The maximum credit starts to phase out at AGI of $200,000 for single parents and $400,000 for married couples. Also, the credit is refundable up to $1,400 if the credit is more than the taxes owed (up to a maximum of 15% of income over $2,500).

III. **Childcare tax credit.** This is different from the child tax credit. It is for the money you spend on childcare so you can work. If your employer offers a pre-tax spending account to let you pay for childcare costs using untaxed income, you should use it. These accounts almost always save you the most money, but they max out at $5,000. If you are already using the childcare account through your employer, you can still claim an additional $1,000 in childcare expenses as a deduction. If you don't have a pre-tax spending account at work, ask for one or make sure you deduct all your costs.

IV. **Credit for older children and adult dependents.** You don't even have to itemize for this one. The child tax credit ends when the child turns 17, but under the TCJA, you can use the Credit for Other Dependents for older children and other adults who qualify. These adult dependents must live with you and not be your spouse. They must be U.S. citizens (or resident aliens, nationals, or Canadian or Mexican residents).

V. Suppose they are your qualifying relative (son, daughter, sibling, half-sibling, step-sibling, parent, step-parent, grandparent, niece, nephew, uncle, aunt, and in-law all qualify). In that case, they might be dependent on you even if they don't live with you. If the person is not related to you, they must live with you to qualify as an adult dependent.

VI. Their total taxable income must be less than the personal exemption would be for the year you claim them. (Note: the TCJA eliminated the personal exemption, but the amount has been retained for this purpose, and for 2021, it stands at $4,300.)

VII. Also, you must be providing more than half of their support. The credit is $500 per dependent adult.

VIII. **American Opportunity Credit.** This credit is for undergraduate students (or their parents if the student is a dependent on the parents' tax return). You can claim a credit of 100% of the first $2,000 in expenses for tuition, fees, and books, and then 25% of the next $2,000, for up to $2,500. Living costs are not eligible. Like many credits, this one is phased out over certain income levels. Suppose your MAGI (modified adjusted gross income) is greater than $90,000 for a single filer or $180,000 for married filing jointly. In that case, you won't be eligible at all. It's partially refundable, which means even if you don't owe any taxes (or you are getting a refund), the IRS will pay you the amount you are eligible for, up to $1,000.

IX. **Lifetime Learning Credit.** This credit is similar to the American Opportunity Credit but is available for graduate, non-degree, and vocational students as well as traditional undergrads. It also applies to tuition, fees, books, and supplies but not living or transportation costs. This one offers up to 20% of the first $10,000 in expenses. The income threshold is lower than for the American Opportunity Credit. It's not refundable, and you can't use both in the same year.

X. In general, tax advisors recommend that taxpayers take advantage of all deductions and credits to which they are legitimately entitled and not let the fear of an audit deter them from using a genuine deduction. If you keep good records, you should be fine.

Section 2
Maximizing accrual: work now, play later

As boxer and entrepreneur George Foreman noted,
"The question isn't at what age I want to retire, it's at what income."

You may dream of retiring at a particular age with specific dreams, but those daydreams will only become realities if you have prepared for them. Your retirement dream might be a life of leisure on a remote beach or mountain cabin. It might involve philanthropic pursuits helping others, or it might be more time to pursue building your stock portfolio. No matter what your goal is, you can achieve it if you dedicate the resources now to making it happen.

The process starts with understanding what you need, what you will have, and building the foundation of what you already have to support what you will need. Planning for retirement is not an easy topic for many people, because it is fraught with confusion and stress. The best way to reduce the level of concern is to increase the level of knowledge. We will discuss pensions, defined contribution retirement plans, other retirement savings, and Social Security.

Defined benefit pensions

It's interesting to note that retirement is actually a modern concept. Until the late 1800s, those who worked for their living expected to continue working until death.

Chapter 3
Retirement income

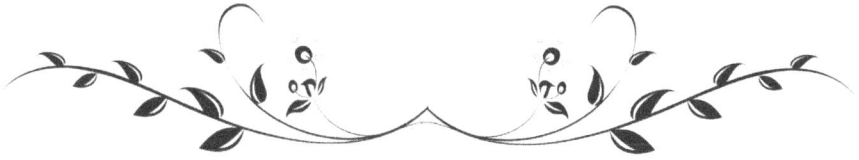

Military pensions started in the Roman Empire and spread after that. Still, most other workers did not begin to be offered a pension until the middle of the 19th century, when some cities started offering retirement or disability income to police and firefighters. The protection then expanded to other municipal employees.

American Express created the first private pension plan in the United States for elderly and disabled workers, beginning in 1875. Fifty years later, 200 large employers in the U.S. offered pension programs (according to the Pension Research Council at the Wharton School of the University of Pennsylvania). Forty-five percent of private-sector employees were covered by a defined benefit pension plan by 1970.

Beginning in 1980, the percentage of private-sector employees with a traditional defined benefit pension plan (which pays a set amount for the lifetime of the retiree, based on years of service to the organization and final or average pay) has steadily declined.

Organizations that do offer defined contribution plans typically employ a formula to calculate the benefit: salary (average or highest) x multiplier x years of service.

Example: $100,000 x 1% multiplier = $1,000 x 30 years = $30,000 annual pension

Example: $120,000 x 1.5% multiplier = $1,800 x 20 years = $36,000 annual pension

Suppose you worked for ABC Corporation for 30 years. If ABC offered a pension, you might be entitled to a percentage of your last annual pay when you retired, plus health care coverage. This program was an excellent repayment for dedicated company service, and it allowed many retirees to enjoy their golden years in quiet prosperity. However, the downside to a traditional pension plan (for the employee) is that the worker has no control over how the funds are invested. The only way the employee can influence the retirement income is to work longer, earn a higher salary, or live longer.

Defined benefit plans costly for employers to maintain

These plans were also costly for the corporations to maintain, and various market forces have encouraged the companies to move away from the traditional pension model.

I. Employee transience. Employees don't stay 30 years with a company these days, and a pension isn't worth anything to a worker who only remains with a company for a few years. The modern workforce isn't faithful to the employer (and the employer isn't loyal to the employee); so, the employer-based pension doesn't make sense.

II. Mergers and takeovers. Suppose Company X, with a bountiful pension plan, is acquired by Company Z, with a less generous plan or no plan. In that case, the two will likely reconcile the conflict in a way that is favorable to the stockholders (the less costly route). The first step in the transformation may be to freeze the plan so that employees are "grandfathered" in to maintain their existing benefit, while new hires are deemed ineligible.

III. Underfunding. Relaxed reporting rules allowed large corporations to use pension assets to finance other goals, and stock market losses contributed to further depletion of pension trust assets. Low interest rates compound the funding problem for companies, especially those with large retiree populations.

IV. High cost. The cost of providing pension access to employees rose from an average of $2.26 per hour per employee in 2008 to $3.74 per employee per hour by 2015 (according to Bureau of Labor Statistics figures). The costs vary considerably by industry and whether or not the company is unionized.

These plans have been replaced in many cases by defined contribution plans such as a 401(k) or 403(b) in which the employee contributes from their earnings. The employer may match some of those earnings and contribute, as well.

According to the U.S. Bureau of Labor Statistics, 4% of U.S. private industry workers have only a traditional defined benefit pension, 13% have access to both types of retirement plan, and 51% of workers have access to only a defined contribution plan through their employer. (The total still leaves 32 percent of private-sector employees with no coverage from any employer plan.)

The workers with coverage by defined benefit plans are almost uniformly union workers, and most are full-time employees. Part-time and non-unionized workers have less access to the traditional pension plan.

However, many government workers still have access to defined benefit pension plans, with almost 90% of full-time state and local workers covered by such programs. Many also have access to defined contribution plans. Federal employees typically are covered by the Federal Employee Retirement System (FERS) and the Thrift Savings Plan, which is similar to a 401(k) plan.

Some local governments have frozen their plans or reduced benefits for newer hires, but in general, access is more widespread in the public sector than for private-sector workers.

Participation in defined benefit plans is high among workers for whom they are available. In most programs, employee contributions are minimal, and the return is guaranteed (unless the fund goes bankrupt). The percentage of workers who contribute to defined contribution plans is notably lower.

Defined contribution plans

There are advantages to a defined contribution plan for both the employer and the employee, but for the worker to gain the benefit, they must participate. Employers have been making changes to encourage participation, like automatically enrolling new hires (who can opt-out rather than making the opt-in decision) and offering more matching or more investment choices. In 2020 U.S. workers had over $6.3 trillion stashed in their 401(k) and equivalent defined contribution plans.

There are different names for the plans depending on the employee it serves:

- ⟩ 401(k) for the private sector
- ⟩ 403(b) for nonprofit and public education employees
- ⟩ 457 for state and local government workers
- ⟩ Thrift Savings Plans for federal employees

For anyone who has access to a sponsored defined contribution plan, most financial planners advise using it. Maximize your contributions, take advantage of the opportunity to reduce your taxable income and grow your earnings tax-free, and never leave an employer match on the table.

Section 401(k) of the Revenue Act of 1978 established the path forward for defined contribution retirement plans. At the time, the idea was groundbreaking, but it initiated the transfer of responsibility for retirement income from employers to workers.

More than 40 years later, these accounts are the primary vehicles for most Americans' retirement savings (besides Social Security).

What are the essential components of a defined contribution plan?

The 401(k) or other qualified defined contribution plan can be identified by the following:

I. Automated contributions. The employee agrees to participate, and contributions of a specified percentage of income are automatically diverted from their pay into the account. Increasingly, employers are adopting an "opt-in" versus "opt-in" approach, which increases participation. "Opt-in" means that employees are enrolled when they join the company at a default percentage contribution unless they make changes or decide to "opt-out."

II. Tax benefits. Employee contributions to the account are not taxed, and earnings in the account are also tax-deferred. The participant owes taxes when they make withdrawals in retirement, presumably with a lower effective tax rate than when they were working and earning a higher income.

III. Employer matches. Many companies match all or part of an employee contribution or contribute a percentage of the worker's pay regardless of whether they participate. Some will match 100% of the first 3% of the salary an employee contributes and then 50% of the next 3%, while others choose different levels. The employer must apply matching to all employees equally for the plan to meet the IRS qualification requirements.

IV. Investment choices. Most 401(k) or similar plans offer the participant various vehicles for investing the funds. Depending on the size of the sponsoring company, choices may be few or many. Some plan administrators offer calendar funds that are designed to balance risk with specific target years of retirement. Others offer particular sector funds, index funds, bonds, money market, global, and many others. If the employer is small, choices may be more limited.

V. High contribution limits. The 2021 limit for an individual with a 401(k) or similar plan is $19,500 (plus an additional $6,500 "catch-up contribution" for workers aged 50 or older). The employer can also contribute, bringing the total to $58,000 in 2021 ($64,500 for workers over 50). Remember, employee contributions are diverted before being taxed and grow tax-free, as well.

What are the disadvantages of defined contribution plans?

From the employee perspective, the main drawback is also the most significant advantage—the control is in the individual's hands rather than the employer's. There is no guaranteed income stream to be anticipated for retirement. The outcome is partly a reward for choices made and partly good fortune. Remember the 2008 crash? Many people lost a great deal of retirement "wealth" during the Global Financial Crisis. The contributions you set aside from your current income may grow steadily only to be devastated by a terribly timed event just before you plan to retire.

Other concerns with these plans are typically related to the plan itself. If the sponsor is small, it may have a program with limited investment choices or high fees. **Even if the plan offered to you seems inadequate, and you don't like the investment options, it is still worth it to contribute enough to obtain the employer match.** That match is guaranteed free money. Passing it up is foolish.

Look at it this way. You work for XYZ Company, and you earn $100,000 annually. If you are eligible for a 401(k) plan in which XYZ will match up to 5% of your income, you should at least contribute that 5%, or $5,000. Let's look at how you benefit from that diversion of income.

⟩ First, you decrease your taxable income. Instead of a taxable income of $100,000, yours is now $95,000. If your overall tax rate is 15%, you just saved $750. (Tax rates used are fictitious, made up to illustrate the example.)

⟩ Second, your employer is giving you $5,000. (Total gain = $5,750.)

⟩ Third, you are investing $10,000. If you get a return of 6% (a reasonable average) a year from now, you will have $10,600 in your account and the $750 you saved in taxes.

⟩ Total one year gain for an investment of $5,000 = $6,350.

⟩ You more than doubled the money, and you won't pay taxes on the gain until you retire and take withdrawals (meaning that you control the timing). You can't pass that up.

⟩ Now, let's rerun the scenario. The employer is still matching up to 5% of your $100,000 income. This time, you contribute the maximum of $19,500 for the year.

⟩ First, you reduce your taxable income from $100,000 to $80,500. Again, assuming your overall net tax rate is 15%, you just saved $2,925.

⟩ Next, your employer is still giving you $5,000.

› Third, now you are investing $24,500. With a 6% return, you will earn $1,470.

› The total one-year gain on your investment of $19,500 is $9,395.

Some 401(k) and similar plans have vesting periods. Any contributions you make to the program always belong to you, along with your earnings. However, the amount your employer contributes may not belong to you until you have been employed for a specific period. If you leave the company before fulfilling the vesting period, you will forfeit the contributions (and earnings) the employer made, at least in part. Usually, this vesting period is five years or less.

Note: some companies (a declining number since the Global Financial Crisis) match their employees' contributions with company stock. This approach is acceptable, but remember to watch your overall concentration in any company, especially the one you work for. Consider diversifying out of the company stock when you are allowed to do so to maintain a balanced portfolio.

What about loans and early withdrawals?

Remember that advice about taking advantage of the opportunity to participate in the 401(k) or similar defined contribution plan? **The corresponding wisdom for this section that a financial planner would offer is to not withdraw from it or borrow from it...unless you have to.**

Retirement Account Loans

Many of these accounts have provisions to allow for loans and hardship withdrawals by employees. Let's take loans first. If your plan allows loans, the IRS has rules that the plan must abide by, limiting the loan amount to either half of what you have vested in the account or $50,000, whichever amount is less. The plan may also set a minimum loan amount and even allow you to have two loans simultaneously. The IRS also requires that the program charge you a fair market interest rate; but remember, you are paying the interest to yourself.

The only cost you pay to the plan is a loan fee, usually at origination and sometimes a quarterly or annual administration fee. The interest payments go back into your account with the loan payments. Usually, you repay the loan through payroll deductions. Some plans require that you stop making contributions to the 401(k) while you have a loan outstanding, but this provision is becoming less common.

The loan term may be anywhere from one to five years (again, individual plans may have other constraints) unless the loan is specifically to provide funds for the purchase of a primary residence, in which case you may be allowed to extend the repayment for a much more extended period.

Here are the positive aspects of a loan from your retirement account:

I. The interest rate won't depend on your credit rating; the plan will set it. Since you are borrowing from yourself, you will usually be approved.

II. Your plan may not require you to explain why you want the money (unless you seek the longer repayment term for a home down payment).

III. There are no income taxes due or withdrawal penalties since you are borrowing, not withdrawing.

IV. There are some clear disadvantages and risks, as well:

V. The money can't grow while it isn't in the account. While you have the money out as a loan for some other purpose, it isn't invested.

VI. The repayments are made with after-tax dollars. Many people suspend or reduce their contributions while repaying a loan (which makes sense, since they needed the money); so, they have no pre-tax dollars going into the account, only the post-tax repayments. This further stalls account growth.

VII. If you leave your job while you have a loan outstanding on the account, the entire balance of the loan is due in 90 days. If you don't pay it in full, it becomes a withdrawal. A withdrawal is subject to income tax and a huge penalty (unless you are 59½). The penalty is 10% of the withdrawal amount, which may wipe out your gains.

With all that said, there are times when that loan may be the best option. Use it sparingly, cautiously, and pay it back quickly.

Hardship withdrawals

In case of specific emergencies, you may be able to withdraw money from your account and not pay it back. The IRS allows the following circumstances:

- ⟩ Down payment for a primary residence or repairs to a primary home
- ⟩ College tuition or other educational expenses
- ⟩ Possible eviction or foreclosure
- ⟩ Medical expenses
- ⟩ Funeral or burial expenses

But within the confines of those choices, the individual plan administrator may allow some and not others as acceptable withdrawal reasons. Many companies require that you suspend contributions for some time (often six months) after the withdrawal and provide documentation of the expense. Your plan may also require that you take out a plan loan first or attempt to borrow from other sources.

You will definitely owe income taxes on the withdrawn amount and the 10% penalty if you are under 59½.

COVID-19 and 401(k) loans and withdrawals

In the CARES (Coronavirus Aid, Relief and Economic Security) Act, Congress included a provision that temporarily allowed withdrawals without the penalty for individuals adversely affected by the coronavirus. To be affected, you or your spouse must have suffered an economic impact such as a job loss. The employer has to approve the change for the plan. While this CARES Act provision expired at the end of 2020, it is still possible to do if the person lives in a major disaster area (the disaster in question must be in addition to COVID-19). So, it's complicated and should be a last resort.

How to invest the 401(k) or equivalent account for the best advantage

Suppose you are contributing faithfully to your tax-advantaged, employer-sponsored retirement account. Good for you. By all accounts, you are the exception to the rule. Americans between 40 and 45 currently have a retirement account balance averaging $14,500—a tiny percentage of what they will need in savings to live on in retirement.

We don't know how much we need, but we strongly (and correctly) believe we don't have enough. We don't know how to get it; so, we ignore the problem, hoping for a miracle. Meanwhile, Social Security continues to provide an ever-smaller amount of the income necessary to fund an adequate retirement. According to a recent article in the *Harvard Business Review*, a median income worker today can expect Social Security (minus Medicare premiums) to cover about 29% of their pre-retirement income. Twenty years ago, that amount was 40%. That doesn't even consider the highly fragile state of the Social Security system as a whole.

BlackRock CEO Larry Fink expressed his concern about retirement this year in a letter to CEOs:

"Many [individuals] don't have the financial capacity, the resources, or the tools to save effectively; those who are invested are too often over-allocated to cash. For millions, the prospect of a secure retirement is slipping further and further away — especially among workers with less education, whose job security is increasingly tenuous. I believe these trends are a major source of the anxiety and polarization that we see across the world today."

People who have invested may be afraid to lose their hard-earned money in the stock market or other investments they do not understand. So, they stick with conservative investments such as bond funds or even cash assets that don't take advantage of the opportunity for growth. If you lost money in the 2008-2009 crash, you may be cringing at the thought of taking on more risk and may, in fact, have your carefully rebuilt retirement account safely stashed in municipal bonds or a money market fund.

Aggressive investing is not for everyone, which is one reason why retirement year funds are so popular. But if your investments are not keeping up with inflation, you aren't winning. As a general rule, the younger you are, the more risk you should take with your portfolio.

The idea is that you can take chances to score big wins, but if you lose, you have time to make up for the losses.

Pundits suggest that you subtract your age from 120 (this number used to be 100, but life expectancy has increased; so, the number has gone up, as well) to determine the percentage of your available funds that you should invest in stocks. So, if you are 40, 80% of your portfolio is in equities, but at 60, the percentage declines to 60, as well.

Risk tolerance and risk capacity

The subtracting from 120 formula is a fundamental approach, and you would be better off making a more detailed determination of your risk tolerance and also your risk capacity. This knowledge will be useful not only as we look at the retirement accounts but later when we dig into other investments.

Risk tolerance is, as it sounds, the amount of risk you are comfortable with—how aggressive you can be and still sleep at night. The calculation should be updated regularly, as it will change with age, personal status, changing goals, and income.

It may actually increase as you achieve a higher level of income rather than decreasing as one might expect. If you are closer to where you want to be than where you started, risking a loss may not be as potentially devastating as when you are just beginning. On the other hand, if you have an unavoidable large expense on the immediate horizon (your child's college tuition, for example), this year might be the year to pull back from some risk.

Risk capacity is what you will have to do to reach your goals—how much you will have to risk to achieve the level you are seeking. Think of this as the final round in *Jeopardy*—if you are in second place, you calculate how much you must risk to win if both you and the champion have the right answer.

Investment choices

Usually, you can't choose individual stocks in which to place your money (with the possible exception of your employer's stock, as mentioned). Still, you should have several mutual funds and exchange-traded funds to pick from. It's crucial to research the fund's success history, because it can vary tremendously. In many cases, the plan administrator will provide you with information about each fund, including the allocation, sector, performance history, and expenses. You want to identify funds with outstanding performance over time and lower costs.

You can target specific industries, such as real estate, energy, financial services, or international companies, or you can choose an index fund, which will mimic the performance of an index like the S&P 500 by benchmarking it. These funds often have excellent performance and low management costs.

If even the thought of choosing between funds makes you sweat, choose a target-date fund. These funds are designed to lead you to the optimal outcome for your planned year of retirement. It will start with more aggressive investments to build earnings; then, as you move closer to the designated year, the fund will gradually shift the balance to safer, more conservative investments that decrease the risk of loss.

Remember, if you choose a target-date fund, do put all your eggs in that basket. It would be best if you didn't hedge this strategy, as it is self-hedging. If you find yourself unsatisfied with the target date fund's direction (too conservative), you may want to choose one with a date further down the road.

What are required minimum distributions?

Once you reach the age of 72, you must begin taking distributions from your 401(k) or similar account. You need to withdraw the required amount by December 31 of the year in which you turn 72 (although there are some exceptions in the first year that can enable a delay until the April 15 tax deadline the following year).

The minimum amount is determined by a specific formula that uses the account balances and your life expectancy factor (published by the IRS). If you are married and your spouse is 10 or more years younger than you, use the IRS Joint Life Expectancy Table instead.

It's essential to pay attention to the minimum distribution requirement, since the penalty for failing to withdraw as required can be 50% of the minimum amount.

What about the Roth 401(k)?

The Roth 401(k) is similar to a regular 401(k) but far less common. The Tax Relief Act of 1997, authored by Senator William Roth of Delaware, created the Roth accounts. We will delve into the Roth IRA later. For both types of Roth account, the salient fact is that the contributions are made with after-tax dollars. Unlike the traditional 401(k), you contribute money on which you have already paid income taxes. However, the earnings on the account grow tax-free, and the distributions are not taxed.

When does this make sense? Contributing to a Roth 401(k)—if this is an option—makes sense if you believe your income tax rate currently is lower than it will be in retirement. If you are at an early place in your career or serving temporarily in a position with lower pay, then this approach may make sense.

Keep in mind that employers may not contribute to a Roth account. If the employer wants to match your contributions, those amounts will go into a traditional 401(k).

Section 3

On your own

Chapter 4
Individual Retirement Accounts (IRAs)

The history of the Individual Retirement Account

As discussed previously, Americans in the middle part of the 20th century were often covered by employer-based pension plans. In the 1960s and early 1970s, many private companies which sponsored those plans began to fail; as a result, many retirees lost their pensions. Partly in response, Congress passed the Employee Retirement Security Act (ERISA) in 1974.

Among the many provisions of ERISA was the creation of the individual retirement account (IRA). The IRA was initially restricted to those workers not protected by a qualified employer-based retirement plan—whether defined benefit like a pension or defined contribution like a 401(k). ERISA allowed such individuals to set aside up to $1,500 annually in a retirement account and deduct the amount from their taxable income, also deferring taxes on the earnings in the account.

The IRA's reach expanded when the 1981 Economic Recovery Tax Act eliminated the eligibility requirement which had excluded those already covered by an employer-sponsored plan, increased the contribution limit, and added the ability to set aside a small amount ($250 annually) for a non-working spouse. Later, the 1986 Tax Reform Act established a phaseout for those taxpayers with higher incomes and access to employer-sponsored plans. The 1997 Taxpayer Relief Act created some limited tax-exempt withdrawal circumstances and introduced the Roth IRA.

The Economic Growth and Tax Relief Reconciliation Act of 2001 increased the contribution limits and added inflation adjustments. It included "catch-up" contributions for taxpayers over 50 who needed to boost their retirement savings. In 2006 the Pension Protection Act made the inflation indexing permanent, allowed some charitable contributions through tax-free withdrawals, and enabled taxpayers to direct the IRS to send refunds directly to an IRA.

Finally, in 2020 the SECURE Act (Setting Every Community up for Retirement Enhancement Act of 2019) made several changes to IRAs, including an increase in the age at which you must begin taking required minimum distributions (RMD). The SECURE Act also repealed the maximum age for making contributions to traditional IRAs and added to the events which qualify for tax- and penalty-free withdrawals.

Traditional IRA

A traditional individual retirement account allows the taxpayer to contribute up to $6,000 in pre-tax dollars to the account annually or their gross compensation, whichever is lower. If the person is 50 or older, the limit is $7,000, and these amounts are adjusted for inflation. If a couple files a joint return, the amounts are doubled. However, only work income is included in the limit on contributions, such as wages, tips, commissions, and income from self-employment. Fellowship and stipend income (such as those paid to graduate students) and alimony are also considered income for this purpose.

Remember that if you have access to a qualified retirement plan through your employer (or you are married to someone who does), then your contributions may not be fully deductible if you have a high income. You can still make contributions up to the limits, and the earnings won't be taxed until you withdraw them, but the contributions could be taxable. Contributions made over the limits are called "excess contributions" if you don't remove them before your tax deadline, and there is a tax penalty for making such contributions.

Where should I set up my IRA?

The good news about starting an IRA is that you can put it wherever you want. The bad news about starting an IRA is that you can put it wherever you want. There are so many options. How do you decide whether to start your IRA with a bank, a credit union, a stock brokerage, or a financial advisor? You can invest in individual stocks, mutual funds, REITs, or a myriad of other possibilities. Compared to the limited choices in an employer-based 401(k), the options can be daunting.

The answer depends in part on how actively you want to manage the investments. If you want to choose the stocks you invest in, choose an account with a low cost structure for executing transactions. If you prefer to have a professional make investment decisions, evaluate financial advisors instead. Remember that we discussed risk tolerance and risk capacity in the section on 401(k) accounts. The same philosophy applies to an IRA. Your investing approach depends on how much risk you are comfortable with and how much you need to take to achieve your goals.

How do I choose the right investments?

You can use mutual funds, index funds, exchange-traded funds, and even individually selected stocks to comprise the equity portion of your portfolio, or you can keep it simple by using a target-date fund. Depending on your overall portfolio's size (including tax-deferred and taxable accounts), you may want to entrust the management to an advisor with fiduciary responsibility or, as a lower-cost option, a robo-advisor.

A "robo-advisor" is an automated investment advisor that will use computer algorithms to manage your accounts. The service will do so without any need for human interaction, although some of the advisor firms also have humans available (for a fee, generally). The robo-advisors typically offer very low management fees and even zero transaction fees. You will need to answer some detailed questions about risk acceptance and financial goals, and then the advisor will set you up with a portfolio of index funds and exchange-traded funds.

Withdrawals and distributions

Withdrawals from your IRA are taxed in the year in which they occur. If you withdraw funds before age 59½, that is an early distribution subject to a penalty of 10% of the withdrawn amount, on top of the tax due. However, the penalty is waived if any of the following conditions are present:

⟩ You are the beneficiary of an IRA account owner who died, and you inherited it

⟩ You are disabled

⟩ You are taking distributions following your anticipated life expectancy

⟩ You are unemployed and over 55 years old

⟩ You are unemployed and using the money to pay medical insurance costs

⟩ You are using the money to fund education costs

- You are using the money (up to $10,000) for a first home purchase or construction
- You are using the money for unreimbursed medical expenses above 7.5% of adjusted gross income (or 10% of AGI if you are under age 65)
- You are a military reserve volunteer converted to active duty
- You are using the money (up to $5,000) for expenses connected to the birth or adoption of a child

IRA loans

There is no provision for taking a loan from an IRA. If you withdraw funds from an IRA, you have 60 days to return the money to the account (or deposit the same amount into another qualified account) to avoid the assessment of taxes and penalties.

Required minimum distributions

Once you reach the age of 72, you must begin taking distributions from your IRA, just as with a 401(k). You need to make the first withdrawal of the required amount by April 1 after the year in which you turn 72, and receive the entire RMD by the end of the year. As with the 401(k) or other defined contribution employer-sponsored account, the required distribution amount can be calculated by dividing the account balance (as of December 31 of the prior year) by the IRA owner's life expectancy. Occasionally, as in 2009 and 2020, Congress will suspend the RMD in response to widespread economic events.

Also, distributions can be made directly from the IRA to a qualified nonprofit and thus excluded from gross income, beginning when the IRA owner is aged 70½.

What about the SEP and SIMPLE IRAs?

The SEP (Self-Employed People) IRA is for self-employed and small business owners with few or no employees. The limits are higher, capped in 2021 at 25% of compensation (or $58,000) but with no catch-up add-on. If you are a business owner funding an SEP for yourself, you must contribute a proportionate amount to an account for each eligible employee. Like a traditional IRA, contributions are tax-deductible, and earnings are tax-deferred until withdrawals begin after retirement.

SIMPLE (Savings Incentive Match Plan for Employees) IRAs are for businesses with less than 100 employees. These are more like 401(k) accounts in that employer contributions are mandatory. The contribution limits for 2021 are $13,500, with a catch-up allowed for those over 50 of an additional $3,000.

How do IRA rollovers work?

Rolling over to an IRA can either be from another IRA or an employer-based plan like a 401(k). Many advisors recommend that when you leave an employer, take your retirement plan with you. In a situation where you are joining a different company with a 401(k) that you can participate in, you may want to roll over the account from your previous employer to the new one.

The preferred method of accomplishing this is directly from one trustee to another, without the funds coming to you. If you have the old account cashed out to you and then reinvest it into the new account, it's complicated. The administrator for the original 401(k) (or any qualified account; keep this in mind for an IRA to IRA transfer, as well) must withhold 20% of the amount for federal taxes due. If you can't replace that amount with money from another source, you will not only be responsible for paying the taxes, but you may also pay a penalty on the withdrawal. If you replace the amount that was withheld, you can recoup the amount when you file your taxes.

The contribution limits do not impact rollovers. They can be made from other IRA accounts or employer plans (if you have separated from employment), including 401(k), 457(b), 403(b), and the Thrift Savings Plan for federal workers.

What is the Roth IRA?

The addition of the Roth IRA was one of the changes made by the 1997 Taxpayer Relief Act. Contributions to a Roth IRA are made with after-tax money, while the gains you make in the account are tax-free. Qualified distributions are not taxed, because the contributions were taxed when you made them initially. Roth IRAs are limited to certain income thresholds. Single filers with 2021 income of less than $125,000 can contribute up to $6,000 (or $7,000 if the individual is aged 50 or more). There is a reduced contribution amount available for single filers with AGI between $125,000 and $140,000 and no eligibility at income over $140,000. For a married couple filing jointly, the respective limits are $198,000 and $208,000.

How are withdrawals from a Roth IRA managed?

There are three kinds of distributions from a Roth IRA:
I. The return of regular contributions made with after-tax dollars
II. Qualified distributions
III. Non-qualified distributions

Because the investor creates a Roth IRA with money on which they already paid taxes, the return of regular contributions from the account to the contributor will not be taxed or penalized.

Qualified distributions, including earnings on the contributions made, will be eligible as such if the following conditions are met:
- The distribution occurs more than five years after the first year in which the investor made the Roth IRA contribution, and one of the following applies:
- The account holder is aged 59½ or older.
- The account holder is disabled.
- The distribution is made to a beneficiary due to the death of the account holder.
- The funds are used to buy, build, or rebuild a first home (limit of $10,000, lifetime).

Non-qualified distributions do not meet the above conditions and are subject to a 10% penalty unless an exception applies. The exceptions are the same as the ones granted to withdrawals from traditional IRAs.

Does a Roth IRA have a backdoor?

Financial advisors may debate the value of "backdoor" contributions to a Roth IRA. This method is only relevant for investors whose income exceeds the allowable threshold for Roth contributions but want to make one anyway. The individual would have also made the maximum allowable 401(k) contribution for the year. It works by contributing to a traditional IRA, then converting that IRA to a Roth. Because the amount directed to the conventional IRA was non-deductible due to the investor's income level, the conversion contains funds that have already been taxed (less any earnings accrued between the initiation of the IRA and the modification).

Investors should be cautious, because this can backfire if the investor has other IRAs or they come into possession of another IRA in the same year (say, they unexpectedly have to roll over an employer-sponsored retirement account or inherit an IRA). Again, this move is complicated, and you should only attempt it with professional guidance.

Can I claim the Saver's Tax Credit?

Remember from the section on deductions and credits that a tax credit is better than a deduction, as it directly decreases the amount of taxes due instead of reducing gross income. The Saver's Tax Credit is a credit, one which is available to low- and moderate-income taxpayers who contribute to a retirement account like a 401(k), IRA (traditional, Roth, SEP, or SIMPLE), or a 403(b) or 457 plan.

If your adjusted gross income is higher than $66,000 for a married couple filing jointly or $33,000 for a single filer in 2021, you can't claim the credit, as it phases out below that. Above that, you won't be able to claim any of it. The credit is non-refundable. Remember, a refundable credit will result in a refund if you don't owe taxes; a non-refundable credit will not.

Should I have a Health Savings Account?

Health Savings Accounts (HSAs) are special accounts that allow taxpayers to set aside pre-tax money for medical expenses. To open an HSA, you must be enrolled in a high-deductible health insurance plan. These plans, which are becoming more widespread as companies struggle to reduce costs, are based on the belief that if people have a higher deductible, they will be wiser about how they use health care. If they are spending their own money on health care, they will do so more judiciously.

To open an HSA, you must be under 65 and have a high-deductible plan. You may have chosen the plan because the premium is lower or because it is the only choice your employer has offered. A high deductible is at least $1,350 for an individual or $2,700 for family coverage. Deductibles may not exceed $6,750 for individual coverage or $13,500 for a family.

While you can't use your HSA contributions to pay for your health care premiums (although your employer may enable you to pay them with pre-tax dollars), you can use the HSA account to pay the deductibles, co-pays, and certain other medical expenses.

HSAs got off to a slow start for a couple of reasons. Some people were reluctant to contribute due to bad experiences with the "use it or lose it" elements of the similar Flexible Spending Account (FSA). While FSAs now have a provision allowing you to roll over a certain amount of unused contributions, the HSA lets you keep the entire unused amount and take it with you if you change employers or retire, unlike an FSA. The limit is $3,500 for an individual and $7,000 for family coverage, and the IRS makes periodic adjustments to the amounts allowed. That maximum includes your contribution and anything the employer adds.

If your employer doesn't offer an HSA but you have a high deductible insurance plan, you can establish an account on your own with a financial institution. You can invest the funds as you choose, and the earnings are not taxed. If you retire and still have unused money in the account, you can use the money tax-free for medical costs. If you need to use the money for other expenses after you retire, you will pay taxes (at your retirement tax level) but not pay a penalty.

Annuities

An annuity is a contract between a single customer (or a couple) and an insurance company. You purchase an annuity, either in a lump sum or by making payments, in return for payments back from the insurance company, either immediately or at a later date. The return payments can be a lump sum for a specific period or for the extent of your lifetime (or both lifetimes, in the case of a couple).

Deferred annuities are more common as instruments to provide income throughout retirement. Guaranteed lifetime income is the most attractive aspect of this type of annuity. The primary downside is a lack of liquidity and control. Investors may hesitate to purchase a deferred income annuity out of concern that they won't get their money's worth if they don't live long enough. Risk sharing is part of how all insurance works, whether it is for your home, car, or retirement income.

There are also other types of annuities, including fixed, indexed, and variable. The investment can be held in a retirement account or separately. Distribution options, required minimum distributions, and tax status depend on how the annuity is set up.

Chapter 5
Social Security

Comedian Pat Paulsen once quipped, "Why should old people get Social Security? They just sit around all day doing nothing."

While that's amusing, more Americans likely agree with Congressman Emanuel Cleaver's view, "Social Security is a covenant that should not be broken."

Before we discuss the details of Social Security, it will be helpful to understand the program's history and dispel some of the more common myths surrounding the Act. The Social Security Act was passed by Congress and signed by President Franklin Roosevelt in 1935. The first taxes were collected for the program in January 1937, and initial payments were disbursed at the same time, although regular benefits were not scheduled until 1940. While the original plan did not include services for disabled individuals or worker's dependents as it does today, the Social Security Act itself involved more than the retirement program. It also created a national unemployment assistance plan and what was known as Aid to Dependent Children.

Social security payments for the spouse and children of a retiree, as well as survivor benefits, were added in 1939, and disability benefits came along in 1956. Medicare, which is the health care arm of the Social Security System, was authorized in 1965 and started operations in 1966.

Numerous myths are attached to the Act's origins, including that it was supposed to be voluntary. This one probably stems from the fact that only about half of American workers were in covered jobs when the program started. But for those who were included, participation was never optional.

Another legend holds that the program's rate of assessment was set "permanently" at 1% and was never to be raised. An examination of the original Act clarifies that Congress meant to establish an increasing schedule and further, the amounts paid were never intended to be deducted from income taxes.

One of the most widespread and heated discussions accompanies the topic of taxation of Social Security benefits. The Social Security Act itself does not address the issue, but during the program's implementation, the Treasury Department ruled that benefits would not be taxed. However, no direct promises on the topic are part of the historical record. In 1983, Congress amended the Act, explicitly authorizing taxing benefits in some circumstances (more on this topic later).

Some other common questions about the Social Security System include these:

Do members of Congress pay into Social Security? Yes. The Amendments passed in 1983 made participation mandatory for all federal employees (with some transitional exceptions), including elected officials.

When did cost-of-living adjustments start? The automatic adjustments were codified by a 1972 law that went into effect in 1975. Previously, Congress periodically approved adjustments.

What is the difference between FICA and Social Security? Nothing, really. The payroll taxes that fund Social Security programs are collected with the authority of the Federal Insurance Contributions Act (FICA) and are, therefore, sometimes called FICA taxes. This includes the taxes for Medicare.

Do the numbers mean anything? Not anymore. Initially, the first three digits had a geographic reference corresponding to where the individual resided when the number was assigned. That system was changed in 2011 in favor of a completely randomized number assignment, which is intended to make the number combinations last longer.

How does Social Security work, and will it be there when I need it?

There is ongoing speculation about the current and future viability of the Social Security system. A report on the system's financial stability, published by the SSA in 2010, declared that if costs continued to rise as expected, the current taxes would only be sufficient to fund 75% of scheduled benefits. The report requested that Congress either reduce benefits or increase the contribution rate to ensure the system's solvency. The existing trust fund would be depleted, and the payments for retirees would then be coming from the contributions of current workers.

The issue has also been discussed in connection with the notion of payroll tax "holidays" that former President Trump was inclined to provide, which temporarily suspended collection of the FICA taxes, alarming some. While this threat seems less imminent now, any recurrence could hasten the system's inability to pay benefits in full.

However, some consumer experts believe it is unlikely Congress would stand by and watch as millions of Americans have their benefits either eliminated or sharply reduced. There are currently several legislative efforts to strengthen the system and preserve the benefits that Americans have paid for.

As tremendous numbers of baby boomers retire, many with inadequate savings, the entitlement program's criticality is evident. It seems unthinkable that our elected representatives could allow its demise, but even with Social Security benefits as part of the mix, many Americans are unprepared for retirement.

How can you best prepare to use Social Security and understand what it will and won't provide for you in retirement?

Understanding how to maximize the benefits you can get from Social Security is a vital step in using the system to your advantage. While you should have (and need) other income streams in retirement, you will want to take full advantage of what is available to you from this program.

Surprisingly, many people do not know what Social Security considers their "Full Retirement Age" or FRA, which is the age at which you receive the standard benefit. If you were born between 1943 and 1954, FRA is 66. If you were born in 1960 or later, it is 67. For those born between 1955 and 1959, the FRA gradually climbs from 66 to 67. You can start benefits a few years before or after the FRA, but taking this action will impact your benefit amount.

How long do I have to work to qualify for Social Security benefits?

To earn a retirement benefit, a worker must collect at least 40 credits. Earning a credit means you worked during a three-month period and made at least $1,470. You can earn four credits in a year; so, you must work at least 10 years (or more, if you work parts of a year) to earn enough credits to qualify. The amount of your benefits is calculated based on your 35 highest-earning years.

The Social Security Administration has excellent online benefit calculators to help you estimate what your benefit will be, using various retirement ages and income forecasts. The current maximum if you retire at full retirement age is $3,113. However, the current maximum for a person retiring at age 70 is $3,895. You may or may not qualify for the maximum, but those figures illustrate the big difference that waiting a few years can make. If that same person retired at 65, the monthly benefit would be lower—25% to 30% lower, depending on your FRA.

Remember, the payments increase by an amount determined by the current inflation rate. The increase is usually small, but it helps. This year the percentage of adjustment is 1.3%, while in 2020 it was 1.6%. In some years there is no increase, but in other years it can be significant.

How does the spousal benefit work?

Spousal benefits can get tricky, but they are designed to protect a non-working or lower-earning spouse both in retirement and after a higher-earning spouse's death. The lower-earning spouse can choose between their benefit or half the value of their spouse's earned benefit.

Example: Joe and Jane are reaching full retirement age together. Joe's benefit will be $3,000 per month. Jane's will be $1,000 per month. Instead of taking her own benefit, she can choose to take an amount equal to half of Joe's, or $1,500. Jane can only do this when Joe is retiring, not before. If Joe dies, Jane can continue receiving his $3,000 benefit but will lose her $1,500 benefit.

You can also obtain spousal benefits based on a former spouse's earnings if you were married for at least 10 years (and you are at least 62 years old and single). As with all benefits, you will get a higher payment if you wait until FRA. It's helpful to note that your ex-spouse does not need to approve or even be aware of your application for the benefits and does not need to file for benefits for themselves. Your filing does not affect their payments or any due to their new spouse, if applicable.

When are Social Security payments taxed?

Social Security benefits are not taxed if that is the only income a retiree has, and that person does not have to file an income tax return. Hopefully, that is not the case, and your other income will lead you to the filing. In that situation, you will determine your IRS "combined income," which is your adjusted gross income (not including Social Security), plus the value of nontaxable interest income and half of your Social Security benefits for the year.

If your combined income is less than $25,000, you will not owe taxes on the benefits. If the combined income is between $25,000 and $34,000, you will need to pay taxes on 50% of the benefit amount, and if the combined income amount is more than $34,000, then 85% of the benefits are subject to income tax. The threshold amounts for married couples are no taxable impact for combined income below

$32,000, 50% between $32,000 and $44,000, and 85% for combined income above $44,000.

What about the earnings test?

Even though there is no means test associated with Social Security benefits (benefits are not determined by financial need, but by the contributions you made to the program), there is a disincentive to collect the benefit while you are still working. The upshot is that you will see your benefit reduced by $1 for every $2 you earn over the threshold (in 2021, that amount is $18,960). It's important to note that this is only true if you start collecting benefits before FRA and only applies to earned income.

If you have investments that provide any amount of income in retirement, those sources of income have no impact on your Social Security payments.

How do I decide when to start benefits?

For most people, waiting until full retirement age (FRA) or longer is the best decision if they don't have a pressing need for the income earlier. Initiating benefits sooner will permanently decrease the amount of the payments you receive and also the payments your spouse gets after your death (if applicable). However, people who don't live until FRA will forfeit the chance to receive benefits if they don't start collecting them sooner; so, your personal and family health history may impact your decision. Perhaps it isn't surprising that only 10% of Social Security recipients delay initial filing beyond the FRA, and many start taking payments sooner, despite the impact on the bottom line amount.

If you claim your benefit early and then change your mind for some reason, you may be able to start over. The Social Security Administration has a withdrawal option you can request within the first year of benefits. If you opted for it, you would have to pay back any benefits you received, but you would be allowed to start over later at the higher benefit level. This choice could be extremely helpful under certain circumstances.

Another possibility is to suspend benefits. If you started receiving benefits at the early retirement age, you can stop at FRA and suspend payments. Without paying anything back, you wait until you turn 70, and during the intervening time you are earning the credit of 8% per year, which makes up for most of what you lost by starting early. It isn't very easy, but it might be the best option in some situations.

How much of my retirement income will Social Security fund?

How much to rely on Social Security depends on several things, including:

⟩ How high your benefit will be (based on your earnings while working)

⟩ How much income you need to afford the retirement you are seeking

For most retirees the benefit should be a supplement, not a sole source of income. The average monthly payment to a retiree is $1,475.13. Will that be enough for you to live comfortably? It probably depends on where you live, whether you have debt (including an outstanding mortgage), and what "comfortable" means to you. According to a Gallup poll in 2019, 57% of retirees say Social Security is a significant source of their income. The Social Security Administration estimates that it constitutes over 90% of available income for 45% of single recipients and 21% of married couple beneficiaries.

What's all this talk about turning Social Security into a big 401(k) plan?

Economists and behavioral psychologists toss out ideas on how to get Americans more "invested" in their retirement. Politicians bandy about plans to salvage Social Security without spending money. Sometimes these possibilities grab headlines, but so far, none have progressed beyond the theoretical stages. It's more likely that small fixes will be made, but it is also possible that benefits will be reduced or the ability to claim benefits before full retirement age will be eliminated.

Section 4
Accumulating Wealth

We have devoted the beginning of this book to learning about the tax system and ways to keep more of what you earn. We outlined the advantages conferred by U.S. policy on income other than earned income, or wages and salary. Now let's examine the path to increasing income from those other sources like investments and real estate. The value of an individual real estate asset or a particular stock may not be comparable over time, but investing in both stocks and real estate are viable means to the accumulation of wealth. All investing carries risk, and every investor determines their individual risk tolerance, as discussed in the section on managing your retirement accounts.

Chapter 6

Investing in Stocks

For the inexperienced investor, the stock market is a mysterious and intimidating place. Everyone wants to find the next Apple or Amazon, hit it big, and be done. It can happen, of course, but don't bet on it. Unless you are the founder or closely associated with a successful start-up's early team, you are unlikely to choose the right stock to go all-in on and reach financial success in one big win. It's like looking for that needle in a haystack. Without trying to discourage you from looking, consider the wisdom of John Bogle, who created the concept of index funds in 1976. He wisely noted that sometimes it's easier to *"buy the haystack."*

History of Stocks

In the 1400s, Antwerp (now Belgium) was the center of trade. Merchants would buy items from others, assuming they could sell them either in the future for more money or use them to create something they could make a profit with.

In 1611 the first known stock was issued by the **Dutch East India Company**. It raised money by offering ownership to investors and paid dividends to the stockholders.

In the United States, government war bonds were officially issued in 1790 and sold to the public for $100 each. Shortly after that, the first **Bank of the United States** (an early version of the Federal Reserve System that failed) issued stocks. Other banks and insurance companies began issuing securities, also, and a disorganized market was taking form.

When a group of the leading participants decided to bring some order and structure to the practice, they wrote and signed what was known as the Buttonwood Tree Agreement, which eventually became the **New York Stock Exchange** (in 1817).

However, the Philadelphia Stock Exchange was actually first founded in 1790. NASDAQ purchased it in 2008.

The Dow-Jones Industrial Average was created in 1896 by Dow Jones & Company, which also founded *The Wall Street Journal*. Founder Charles Dow thought the public would benefit from having a simple way to visualize whether the stock market was going up or down. The DJIA (Dow Jones Industrial Average) initially used 12 stocks for its benchmark but now has 30, including Coca-Cola, Microsoft, Boeing, and Apple.

Companies are replaced on the DJIA if they are acquired, suffer significant misfortune, or if changes would better reflect the U.S. economy. For example, in March 2015 DJIA removed AT&T in favor of Apple, and in 2018 General Electric (which was the last holdover from the original 12) was replaced with Walgreens Boots Alliance. All included companies must trade on the **NYSE** (New York Stock Exchange) or **NASDAQ** (National Association of Securities Dealers Automated Quotations).

Other indexes exist, some of which are considered more reliable, and we will discuss them in greater detail shortly. It is helpful to develop an understanding of the indexes for several reasons, including investing in exchange-traded funds. Another well-known index, the **Standard & Poor's 500 Index**, is a market capitalization weighted index of the 500 largest publicly-traded U.S. companies. The index was created in 1941.

Notable crashes:

1929: After The Roaring 20s pushed the markets to high levels on the strength of leveraged speculation, the market crash destroyed investors and spurred reforms. Sixteen million shares were traded on October 29, 1929 (known as Black Tuesday), leading to the economic ruin of thousands of American investors and the loss of billions in wealth. It took 10 years for the United States to recover from the Great Depression.

The cause of the crash was identified as the rapid expansion of the market, fostered by speculation that only seemed reckless in hindsight. Unemployment was high, and banks were excessively leveraged. Within a couple of years, many banks collapsed. By 1933 nearly one-third of the U.S. workforce was unemployed. In some areas it was far higher. The depression was finally relieved by the twin forces of the New Deal and World War II.

The New Deal included relief in the form of jobs and support for farmers. It also provided reform with the Glass-Steagall Act, the National Labor Relations Act, and, of course, the 1935 Social Security Act.

1987: The October 19 downturn known as Black Monday was probably fueled by portfolio insurance, which is a system designed to protect against risk by short-selling stock futures to hedge a portfolio. The automatic trading systems are designed to sell when specific prices are recognized so that no human interaction is needed. That pushed prices continually lower, causing a vicious cycle of stop-loss orders. Both the DJIA and the S&P 500 lost more than 20% of their value that day, although some of the loss was quickly recovered.

There were hints of a coming bull market and concerns about program trading. However, similar drops may still be possible in the future, even with the addition of circuit breakers and other protective measures.

2008: The collapse of mortgage-backed securities and the housing market bust destroyed trillions of dollars in value. Americans lost nearly $10 trillion in wealth as their retirement accounts became nearly worthless and the equity in their homes disappeared. Simultaneously, unemployment peaked at 10% in October 2009.

Deregulation of the financial services industry was one of the seminal catalysts of the 2008 Global Financial Crisis. The Glass-Steagall Act, passed in 1933, had several essential banking reforms:

It separated commercial banking from investment banking.

It created the Federal Deposit Insurance Corporation, protecting consumers from insolvent banks.

But in 1999, the Gramm-Leach-Bliley Act repealed the portion that prohibited commercial banks (those that provide services we think of as retail banking, like checking accounts and home loans) from competing in investment services such as initial public offerings and merger and acquisition activity. This "modernization" gave banks leeway to use consumer deposits to invest in derivatives. A derivative is a contract that obtains its value from the agreed-upon value of a group of assets. The price of the product comes from fluctuations in the investment. At the time, Enron was using derivative trading to hedge its futures exchanges.

Like energy derivatives, mortgage-backed securities are priced based on the value of the mortgages that comprise the bundle. The value of the bundle is determined using a formula that considers several factors, including the amount of the mortgages, the monthly payments, the quality (likelihood of repayment), and the estimated future value of the collateral (the real estate assets).

The bank that gave the mortgage to the consumer sold the loan to the hedge fund and continued making more mortgage loans. The original lender could either collect the payments (known as servicing) or sell that right to another company. Either way, the payment was part of the amount going to the investor; so, the bank or servicer just collected and passed it along.

To add to the complexity, the investors could protect themselves against the mortgage default risk by buying credit default swaps sold by insurance companies. All these factors continued to increase the demand for the MBS (mortgage-backed securities), which in turn increased the availability of mortgage loans.

Added to this, the rise of adjustable rate mortgages and interest-only loans (to accommodate those who could not afford the full payment) created ever higher demand for mortgage loans, which in turn drove up housing prices. As interest rates rose through the early 2000s and those adjustable loans started to reset, the borrowers could not afford their monthly payments, and things began to go haywire. Home supply caught up with demand, prices began to drop, and suddenly many homeowners were "under water" and could not sell their homes for enough to pay off the mortgage they owed. The resulting bubble exploded into the financial firms that were reliant on the derivatives and financial instruments tied to those mortgages' securitization.

The 2010 Dodd-Frank Wall Street Reform and Consumer Protection Act responded with tighter regulations on banks and other lenders as well as insurance companies and credit rating agencies. The Volcker rule was a crucial part of Dodd-Frank, placing restrictions on what investments banks could make with their accounts and limiting certain hedge fund activities. However, actions by the Office of the Comptroller of the Currency and the FDIC have recently begun to back away from those restrictions.

Understanding the terminology

In order to approach the stock market with confidence, it will help to develop familiarity with the standard terms investors use. Here are some of the most important.

Annual Report. Detailed information about a company's financial status, prepared yearly to inform current and potential investors about the company.

Arbitrage. This practice takes advantage of the difference in price for a stock sold on more than one exchange. If you can buy it for $1.00 and sell it for $1.25 somewhere else, the $0.25 per share is an easy profit.

Averaging down. Buying more shares of a stock while the price is dropping. If you believe the price will recover, this reduces the average price you pay for the stock. For example, if you bought 100 shares at $100, and now the stock is selling for $75, but you believe in the long-term value, you buy 100 more shares at $75 each. Now your basis in the stock is $87.50, and you can make a profit at a lower price point.

Bear market. Stock market value is falling. Phrases like "Bears are taking over the bulls" mean investors who believe the market will drop are gaining in number.

Blue chip stock. A share of a well-capitalized, usually profitable company with a record of paying dividends.

Bull market. The market value is rising. This is the opposite action of a bear market.

Bid/ask/spread. The bid is the price a trader is willing to pay for a stock; the ask is the amount the seller wants to receive; and the spread is the difference between the bid and the ask.

Day trading. This traditionally meant investors who buy and sell a stock within the same trading day. The definition has expanded somewhat to include individuals trying to make money quickly by churning stocks.

Dividend. A distribution of income that many companies pay out to shareholders, often on an annual or a quarterly basis. Not all publicly traded companies pay dividends, but their stockholders follow the distributions closely.

Exchange-traded funds. These mutual funds track an index. Unlike mutual funds, ETFs trade throughout the day, like stocks. There are often tax advantages to buying ETFs due to the passive income.

Going long. This is betting the stock price will increase and you will make a profit.

Hedge fund. An investment fund that takes substantial risks in its approach. Often the fund will take positions that generate positive returns whether the market is up or down.

Initial Public Offering. This is the first sale of stock by a company. Usually, a start-up will issue a public offering when it has reached a specific size or needs more capital to expand than it can obtain in the venture capital markets or when the management team is ready for other reasons. There is a lot of strategy involved in the timing and the pricing of the IPO. The **Securities Exchange Commission regulates IPOs.**

Leverage. Using leverage means buying stock with borrowed money. For example, if you want to buy 100 shares of a stock that costs $100 per share, you need $10,000. If you only have $2,000 and your broker will loan you the rest, you are using leverage. If the stock price increases to $150 per share, you have increased your ability to profit from the rise by using leverage. If, however, the stock price drops and you don't have the money to cover the debt, you have a problem. That's why using leverage is risky. You use a **margin account** to transact these purchases and sales.

Limit order. This is an instruction that a buy or sell is to be completed at a certain price. For example, if ABC stock falls to a cost of $100 per share, buy 100 shares. If XYZ stock reaches a price of $100 per share, sell 100 shares.

Liquidity. How easy it is to sell a stock (or other investment).

Market capitalization. This is what the market thinks a company is worth.

Market order. Buy or sell at the market (current) price.

Moving average. The average price of a stock share during a specific period of time (30, 50, or 200 days, for example) is the moving average. During the same period, you may hear of the high and low prices for the stock.

Mutual fund. An investment account that manages your money by buying and selling stocks. The fund managers report on gains and losses and often focus on particular sectors.

Sector. The sector is another word for the industry. Some investors like to specialize in an industry like energy, financial services, or real estate.

Short selling. This is betting that the price of a stock is going down. You essentially borrow shares for a specific time through your margin account. You must return it by the expiration date whether or not the price has done as you expect. Like using **leverage**, this is risky.

How to invest in the stock market

As much attention as we pay to the markets, many Americans aren't personally invested in stocks. In 2020 a slight majority of Americans either directly or indirectly (as part of a mutual fund) owned stock. The bulk of those invested only have retirement fund access to the market, while approximately 15% (according to available data from the Federal Reserve) own individual stocks directly. Not surprisingly, families with higher household incomes are more likely to report stock ownership than those with lower incomes.

Having disposable income is necessarily a prerequisite to investing. One must pay the rent, utilities, and food bills before using money to make more money. Although no one knows where the "rule" originated, it is said of both gambling and investing that you should never risk money you can't afford to lose. On the other hand, Warren Buffet, widely revered for his success in investing, offers instead:

"Rule No. 1: Never lose money. Rule No. 2: Never forget Rule No. 1."

Keep it simple with investment funds

In many ways, it is easier today than ever been before for anyone with the desire and any amount of available capital to invest in stocks. Remember the previous reference to John Bogle and the Vanguard Index Fund? Bogle and his fund revolutionized the structure of mutual funds by eliminating outside owners and significantly reducing costs. The index mirroring concept provided a stable, reliable return on investment for investors who did not have to accumulate the knowledge to choose their own stocks or rely on advice from brokers.

Investing in a fund reduced the need for individual transactions, further lowering the cost of investing. Investors could easily "buy the haystack" and benefit from the profitable needles hidden inside. As a reminder, an index fund is designed to match the chosen index's performance without active fund management. This structure allows the fund to operate with lower costs. Some large funds currently charge almost nothing to investors (one literally has no expense fee). Other advantages of index funds include:

> Stable growth. Like the indexes they mirror, the funds will fluctuate, but most offer excellent long-term returns.
> Low risk. Index funds are inherently diverse due to the large number of companies in the mix. This mix guarantees lower concentration and less risk.
> Fewer taxable transactions. The funds do not make as many transactions, causing less taxable activities for the investor.

If you want to invest in an index fund, you have many options for doing so. The S&P 500 is probably the most popular. Other indexes used for funds include the DJIA, the NASDAQ composite index, the Russell 2000, and the S&P SmallCap 600. There are also international indexes such as the MSCI and bond funds.

The profitability of investing in an index fund is hard to overstate. Many funds have achieved annualized returns of 10% over the last 30 years. It is a reliable way for people with limited time and limited funds to enjoy the benefits of appreciation that are available in the stock market, with little downside.

What about mutual funds?

One difference between an index fund and a traditional mutual fund is that the index fund is set up to mirror the index's performance, while a mutual fund seeks to beat the returns of any index. The mutual fund, actively managed by fund investment managers, have higher expenses and, thus, higher fees. The investor pays for the expertise of the fund manager and analysts who do the research that leads to the decisions the fund makes to buy and sell the stocks in the fund. Those higher expenses cut into the returns the fund makes.

Looking at average costs, index funds focused on U.S. stocks have an average expense ratio of 0.09%, while similar mutual funds charge 0.68%. That is a tremendous cost difference that can easily outweigh any superior fund performance. In most sectors, however, the index funds rival or outperform their mutual fund competitors, making a case for index funds even stronger. There is an exception for investors looking for funds in the emerging markets and high yield (junk bond) categories in which the returns for managed funds are superior.

What is an ETF (exchange-traded fund)?

An ETF is like a mutual fund but has some things in common with the index fund, as well. ETFs track a fund or sector, commodity, or another benchmark like an index fund. They are traded throughout the day as opposed to mutual funds, which only change at the trading day's close. Like index funds, ETFs offer diversification and risk management as well as cost control. They also have advantages from a tax perspective, since the investor only incurs a capital gain when they sell the fund, not when the fund makes transactions.

Direct stock ownership

Perhaps, despite the seeming advantages of investing in the stock market by letting someone else do all the work while you go sailing, you have your heart set on building your own portfolio (and cashing in on that big winner). How do you buy and sell individual stocks? There are many ways to answer that; so, let's begin with the practical.

How to buy stocks

Like most other transactions, buying and selling stock has become accessible to almost everyone and in ways we might not have imagined just a decade ago. You can sign up with an online broker in minutes and make your first purchase of whatever stock you choose almost as easily as placing an order with your favorite online retailer. If your favorite online retailer is Amazon (AMZN) and you invested $10,000 in the stock when it went public on May 15, 1997 at $18 per share, your stake would have been worth over $12 million by May 2020.

As mentioned, that kind of value increase is improbable, but it's what many investors dream of. The convenience and low cost of online trading is clearly a positive occurrence that should continue to bring access to the stock market for an ever-larger group of potential investors. As a cautionary tale, though, everyone should be responsible for understanding what they are "signing up" for. The recent surge in popularity of "meme" stocks and some of the tangential problems that accompanied novice traders' introductions to the market demonstrate that investing is not foolproof.

Another option is to use a traditional stockbroker, a professional who not only executes the buy and sell orders for you but also supplies you with investment advice and recommendations (hopefully, "buy Amazon at $20 per share"). The broker charges a fee, which can be a percent or a flat rate, for the work they do for you. Not surprisingly, the share of transactions managed by traditional brokers continues to decline. With all the resources available to investors, few are willing to pay for the luxury of having someone else handle their transactions.

Which stocks to buy?

Whether you are buying through an online brokerage or a personal broker, choosing the stocks in your portfolio is the hard part. Many investors have a philosophy or strategy about the companies they choose, while others go with an emotional or "seat of the pants" approach. One of the most successful and renowned investors of all time is the so-called "Oracle of Omaha," Warren Buffet. In addition to his rules about not losing money, Buffet offers plenty of other investing advice. He firmly adheres to a holding strategy, resisting the impulse to sell a stock when a company is going through hard times. In fact, he views those downturns as opportunities. He always evaluates the long-term prospects of the company before investing and requires of himself that he write down valid reasons why he considers a stock worth the price he is about to pay.

How do Buffett and other savvy investors evaluate the companies in which they invest? By analyzing the companies' operating conditions, particularly the financial situation. Investors will review the cash flow, earnings, and equity statements of a company to determine the organization's health. All publicly traded companies publish their financial details so that investors and regulators can examine them for risks and potential.

You can also find an advisor you trust to evaluate companies and follow their suggestions. Analyzing a company's price-to-earnings ratios, retained earnings, debt levels, and so on isn't as easy as it sounds.

What about dividends?

Some companies pay dividends or distributions to shareholders from their profits. Dividends can be in cash or additional stock shares. A company can only issue these dividends from retained earnings, which might have otherwise been reinvested into the company; so, there is controversy about whether dividends are good or bad in the long term. However, some investors have a strong preference for buying stock in dividend issuers.

Earlier, we mentioned the Dividend Aristocrats, which have increased their dividends annually for at least 25 consecutive years. Other dividend-paying stocks like Verizon, Microsoft, and Apple have not paid as frequently, choosing in some years to reinvest earnings into growth, but which would still qualify for many advisors' "buy" lists.

You may want to reinvest the dividends into additional stock unless you rely on the distributions as income. Whether you reinvest or take the dividend as cash does not impact the taxable nature of the payment. As discussed in the earlier section, dividends are not taxed for many taxpayers and are at a lower rate for almost all.

If you are inclined to invest in dividend stocks, here are some things to look for:

- ⟩ Consistency. If a company's philosophy is to pay the dividend, it's essential that it can maintain it.
- ⟩ Payout ratio. The amount the company pays shouldn't be too high a percentage of earnings per share, or it may not be sustainable.
- ⟩ Competitive advantage. Does the company have what it needs to maintain its edge?

How does a stock split?

A stock split is, as it sounds, the division of a single share into two, three, or more. The split isn't as popular as it once was, and technically it doesn't change the value of a share or the market capitalization of a company. Still, it is often a recognition that the value of the business is increasing. For example, if XYZ Company shares rise in value from $10 to $100 and then split in a 1:2, the investor now has two shares worth $50 each rather than one share worth $100. There is no change in overall value, but the shares often continue to rise, and the investor now has more.

However, some companies are avoiding the split regardless of the continued rise in their stock price. This tactic may make the shares less available to small investors, but with the popularity of mutual and index funds, investors don't need to buy individual shares independently.

There is also a move known as a reverse split in which a company will consolidate shares (if you owned 10 shares valued at $10 each, you would now own just 1 valued at $100), but this is far less common. One motivation is to disguise a dropping stock price, perhaps to avoid delisting by an exchange.

Stock options

Employee stock options can be part of a compensation package, either at a small start-up or at a more established company. The options are included along with your salary and other benefits. They are intended to encourage you to stay with the company for a period of time to reap the reward that comes (hopefully) with the options. You have the opportunity to buy the stock at a specified price, usually at a date in the future. The options may vest (become available to you) over time or all at once.

Suppose you join XYZ Company, and you get 10,000 stock options that will vest in increments of 2,500 annually after one year with a "strike price" of $10. In other words, one year from the grant date you can buy 2,500 shares of company stock at $10 each. (If the company is not yet public, it's a bit different.) When the vesting date arrives, you have earned money if the stock price is above $10.

Let's say the stock price is at $15 on your first vesting day. You can buy 2,500 shares for $10 each if you have $25,000 available. Then you own the shares and can hold them, give them away, or do whatever you want. If you don't have $25,000 available to buy the shares, you can execute an "exercise and cover," which involves selling enough of the shares to pay for the transaction and keeping the rest. Or, if you are looking for the cash, you can complete an "exercise and sell" in which you buy and sell, retaining the profits (minus commissions, if any, and taxes owed). The taxes owed will depend on several factors, including the type of stock option, the length of time you held the stock before selling it, and your other income.

Stock options generally have an expiration date. If the stock price does not reach the strike price before the expiration date, you would not be gaining anything by exercising the option. If you believe the stock will climb past the strike price, you can exercise and hold, which helps with the capital gains holding period (if applicable).

Should I invest in bonds?

Bonds are fixed-income investments that are generally considered low-risk and low-return. There are government bonds and corporate bonds, and in most, the interest rate remains the same throughout the term. Financial advisors agree that bonds have a place in your portfolio, but the share of your holdings should be small, especially before retirement.

In the past, a split of 60% stocks and 40% bonds was a standard recommendation, but that is currently considered too conservative by most advisors. The stock market returns will almost always be so much better than what you can earn buying bonds. Those who over-invest in bonds run the risk of running out of money to pay for their retirement, especially as we all live longer. Younger investors should forego bonds altogether, and mature individuals should not overdo them.

How to survive the next crash

A market correction is a decrease of between 10% and 20% in the stock market, often in response to an economic or political event. Twenty-seven corrections occurred since World War II, and most lasted only a few weeks or a couple of months. A bear market is a decline of greater than 20%, and a crash is defined as a rapid and unanticipated drop.

The stock market is up, and then it is down. It will be a bear and then a bull. Successful investors do not sell when values are down and do not buy when prices are up. To prosper through the ups and downs, consider these precautions:

Asset balance. Keeping much of your portfolio in the stock market is fine if you have the patience to leave things alone when the market is down. Stocks are long-term investments, and it's rarely wise to react to market fluctuations. But as you get closer to retirement, it's crucial to shelter a more significant percentage of your assets from risk. Remember the discussion from earlier about risk tolerance and risk capacity. Find the balance for your situation.

Available cash. If you have a fund to take advantage of bargains, then a downturn in the market seems more like an opportunity than a disaster. Keep some money handy to buy a stock you have had your eye on when the price tumbles.

Dividend stocks. Having some reliable dividend producers can take the sting out of a reduced value in your portfolio.

Diversity. If you are careful about the mix of stocks (either by buying individual companies or focusing on funds), you will be protected from the worst of the market swings.

Section 5
Real Estate

John D. Rockefeller claimed, "The major fortunes in America have been made in land." Andrew Carnegie agreed, stating, "Ninety percent of all millionaires become so through owning real estate."

Investing in real property may not be the only way to accumulate wealth. Indeed, those who start companies in the tech industry have found an alternate path. Still, it is one of the most reliable and frequent routes to affluence. But there is no single path. Real estate includes many choices, from single-family property to multi-family investing, commercial assets, and fractional investments. Any investor may start with any of these and diversify to include as many as they want.

As with the stock market, it will be helpful to share some definitions of key terminology for real estate investors before we start digging in. Understanding these terms will provide a foundation for the concepts that come after:

Appraisal. An independent determination of a property's value, usually arranged by the lender.

BRRRR. In the jargon of those who deal in "fixer-uppers," this refers to "Buy-Rehab-Rent-Refinance-Repeat," which is a system of building a rental portfolio.

Buyer's Agent. The real estate agent representing a buyer seeking to purchase a home. Assists with finding the home, negotiating the deal, and arranging for the inspection, appraisal, and other services. The agent receives a portion of the commission.

Carrying Costs. Expenses the investor must plan on from the time they purchase until they sell (such as a mortgage, interest, taxes, insurance, and utilities).

Cash flow. Net income of a property (rent minus ownership and operational costs).

Closing. Meeting at which a real estate transaction is finalized.

Closing costs. The fees associated with the sale of a property, including commissions, taxes, title insurance, appraisal, and transfer documentation. These costs average 2-5% of the property sale price.

Comparables. Similar homes or properties near the one being bought, with recent selling prices agents and appraisers can use to validate the value.

Contingency. Conditions that must be resolved (by the buyer or the seller) before a transaction can close.

Depreciation. A tax treatment, but also the decrease in value of a property over time. Buildings and other improvements depreciate; the land does not.

Equity. The difference between the current mortgage and the market value of a property.

Flipping. A strategy of buying an asset, putting some money into improvements, and selling it quickly for a higher price.

Foreclosure. The repossession of a property by a financial institution when an owner does not make timely mortgage payments.

LTV (loan-to-value). The ratio of the loan compared to the value of the asset. If you make a 20% down payment, the LTV is 80%.

Listing Agent. The real estate agent representing a home seller. The person must be a licensed real estate agent or a broker. Assists the home seller with finding buyers, setting the sales price, negotiating with buyers, and overseeing the transaction. Usually works on a commission, paid only if the home is sold.

Motivated seller. A property owner who has a reason to sell—perhaps they are in danger of foreclosure or nearing retirement. These owners are sometimes agreeable to lower offers.

Property inspection. An independent determination of the property's condition.

Rental agent. Can be either a professional who helps renters find suitable dwellings to rent or one who helps landlords find qualified tenants. Will be paid by the party for whom the agent is working.

ROI (return on investment). The net profit of investment property compared to the cost. Higher ROI is better.

Short sale. If a property is mortgaged for more than the current market value (also referred to as being under water), the owner may sell it for less than the amount they owe. This act requires the approval of the lender.

A common place for beginners to start is by turning a residence into a rental. Suppose you bought a home, watched the house appreciate in value, and then used that equity to finance the purchase of another property. You are now a real estate investor.

Chapter 7
Residential Real Estate

Starting with a rental

Let's look at how this can work. If you use the equity (which is the ownership or value you have) in your primary residence as the down payment on an additional single-family home, you can rent out the home you already owned or the one you purchase. Backing up for a moment, how do you get equity, and how do you get access to it? Suppose you bought your primary residence (the home you purchase to live in) for $400,000. If you made a 20% cash down payment using your savings, you already have 20% equity in the home.

As you make payments, your equity increases. Often, the home's value in the market is also increasing, and your equity rises that way, as well, often more quickly. Keep in mind that while home prices usually rise, they can and do drop, and sometimes they drop very quickly (as during the Global Financial Crisis). But in this scenario, the equity has increased, and you can now use that value as your down payment on another property. Using earned equity as a down payment for the next property is leverage, and leverage is what makes real estate so attractive to investors.

Interestingly, real estate does not generate the same level of returns as stocks do (adjusting for inflation and the increase in home sizes). But while it is not considered prudent in most cases to purchase stock with leverage, it is commonplace, even expected, in buying real estate. Here is why leverage multiplies the impact of your investment:

If you buy something for $100 and its value increases by 3%, you have earned $3.

If you buy something worth $500, using $100 of your own money and borrowing $400, and the value increases by 3%, you have earned $15 (minus whatever it cost you to borrow the $400).

That is a big difference. If someone was paying you to use that item at the same time, you are earning enough to pay for the borrowing costs, and the extra appreciation you got from the leverage is all profit.

If we look at this example in real estate terms, it makes even more sense. You take equity from your primary residence and leverage it to buy a second property. That second property rises in value, increasing your equity both in the portion you put the down payment money in and the part you own through borrowing. At the same time, you rent out the property to cover the cost of the mortgage and other expenses.

Also, as a real estate investor, you gain access to numerous tax advantages. Because owning real estate is your business, and you are pursuing it to make money, you can deduct many expenses from the income the pursuit generates. Keep in mind the business deductions we discussed for small companies earlier, and factor those in, as well.

Investing in single-family real estate is considered less risky than investing in equities. It can be an excellent source of passive income and tax deductions, and the investment nearly always increases in value over time. On the other hand, real estate is not liquid. That means you may not be able to dispose of it quickly if you have a sudden need for cash, and there are risks.

The primary risks involved with real estate investing are related to tenants and properties. If the building is not rented out, the expenses (carrying costs) continue while the income stream dries up. Potentially worse, a bad tenant can harm your investment by damaging the property. Regardless of tenant-caused problems, the property will need repairs and maintenance. The unexpected failure of significant systems is part of the reality of owning investment property, just as it is part of being a homeowner.

Let's say your carrying costs on a single rental are $3,500 per month, and you usually rent the unit for $4,000. You also calculate a monthly value of $750 in tax benefit (this is a hypothetical formula); so, the total overage is $1,250. That's a nice difference. But if the unit is vacant for several months, the costs add up quickly.

Is a property manager worth it?

Hiring a property management company to handle the renting, rent collection, interaction with tenants, and other day-to-day aspects of property investment is a decision you may make at some point in your journey. The timing depends on your appetite for the ordinary chores of being a landlord and the size of your portfolio. If you have a small number of single-family homes or duplexes you rent out, you may be able to keep up with the tenant demands if you are a decent handyman or don't mind taking the weekend calls about clogged plumbing and broken appliances.

If your collection of properties grows large enough, you may not be able to manage the demand, and you may not want to. Indeed, if you are a part-time investor and working another job simultaneously, it won't be easy to be responsive to the tenants' needs. It may be logical for you to hire a company to handle the details. Or you may choose to hold on to the parts of managing you have an affinity for and outsource the ones that aren't your strong suit. For example, you can pay a leasing company to check the credit and references of potential tenants (staying in compliance with fair housing requirements is crucial), but once the tenant is in place, keep the job of collecting rent for yourself. In such an arrangement, you would likely pay the property manager on a fee-for-service basis rather than a more traditional percentage of the rent.

You may want to think of the self-management to property management decision as more of a spectrum than a single choice. You may decide to retain some aspects of the work and hand over others or give control over all the details to a professional. Suppose you go to a property manager for the overall administration of your tenant selection, retention, rent collection, property maintenance, and so forth. In that case, the cost can equal 5-10% of the gross income from rent.

What should I look for in a property manager?

If you decide to engage a property manager, ensure you are getting value for that percentage of income you are relinquishing. The manager you hire must be fully versed in current federal, state, and local housing laws and have demonstrated experience with the size of housing unit you specialize in. Later we will talk about multi-family housing and the special considerations in large complexes.

Several associations train and credential property managers, including the National Association of Residential Property Managers, which offers certificate designations to members, recognizing training and expertise levels. You may want to begin with these organizations as you look for a high-quality manager. The contract with the manager is crucial as is confirmation that they have appropriate insurance, including general liability, property-casualty, and errors and omissions (E&O).

Can I make money flipping houses?

You can probably make more money flipping houses than flipping burgers or pancakes, but you are more likely to accumulate wealth for the long term with a buy and hold, rent and repeat strategy. House flipping sounds like an easy way to make a killing in real estate, but by all reliable reports, it isn't that lucrative.

If you buy a flip for $200,000, spend $40,000 on renovations and repairs, have $20,000 in acquisition and disposition costs, you have to sell it for over $260,000 just to break even. You have to know the market very well to be sure you can do that. If you are making mortgage payments on that house while you try to sell it, the pressure may be too much. Most flippers use cash so they can wait for the right offer. Still, the average profit is in the $20,000 range in most markets. That doesn't mean you won't get lucky and make $100,000 on one flip, but you may lose $100,000 on the next one.

Flippers may refer to the 70% rule. It means they will buy a house for 70% of the forecasted value after repairs minus the cost of getting to that value. If the home is anticipated to sell for $100,000 after $30,000 in repairs, the acquisition price should be no higher than $40,000.

Flipping is a decent sideline for some investors. Those investors share the following characteristics:
1. Access to cash
2. Highly tuned knowledge of the local real estate market
3. Renovation skills or excellent industry contacts

Some real estate agents flip houses. Having a real estate license is helpful, since you can save money on the properties' acquisition and disposition, and you have easier access to information about available homes. Real estate professionals may also have the scheduling flexibility needed to oversee a house undergoing renovation while simultaneously working in their clients' interests.

Tax advantages of real estate income

As previously discussed, the income from real estate investments is treated differently from the income you earn from salary, wages, and commissions. If you are an investor, you are most likely going to need a tax advisor, and this is not intended to provide tax advice. But it can help to visualize some of the beneficial treatment and potential opportunities you can look forward to.

The rent you receive from your tenants is income. If you rent out a house for $2,000 per month, that is $24,000 per year income to you (assuming it is occupied and rent is paid each month). If you receive a month of rent in advance, you count that in the year you receive it. A security deposit may or may not be income. It depends on whether it will be designated as the last month's rent or returned to the tenant if not required to pay for damage to the home.

Also, include in your income any payments a tenant makes that they deduct from the rent. For example, if the tenant pays the water bill on your behalf and subtracts that amount from the rent, that is technically rent, and you count it as income. If the tenant is responsible for paying the water bill in addition to the rent, you don't count the water bill as income to you. Services must be valued as income. If your tenant performs repairs in exchange for part of the rent, you must report that as income at the value of the work done.

To offset the income, you get to deduct expenses. The deductible expenses include:

> Mortgage interest
> Property taxes
> Operating expenses
> Depreciation
> Repairs

How does depreciation work?

Notice that while the above list of deductible expenses includes mortgage interest, it does not include the mortgage itself. That's where depreciation comes in. Just like a big corporation writes off (depreciates) its investment in equipment over time, you write off your investment in the asset (the dwelling unit) over the course of time. In the case of a home, the IRS specifies that the useful life is 27.5 years.

You can claim the depreciation of the building used for rental income (or any other asset that has a useful life of more than one year). The land is not depreciable, because it does not lose its ability to be used. For that reason, you must subtract the value of the land from the value of the dwelling when you determine your **cost basis**. The cost basis is what you paid for the property plus some other fees. You can include recording costs, transfer fees, title insurance, and property taxes but not insurance premiums, mortgage insurance, mortgage points credit report, or appraisal costs.

Usually, the tax assessment will distinguish the value of the land from the value of the improvements or buildings. The cost basis can be adjusted if you make improvements and for specific other causes.

Since the depreciation takes place over 27.5 years, you would write off the cost at a rate of 3.636% each year for the length of time you continue to own and use the property as a business asset. If you use the property for less than a full year, you will prorate the depreciation amount. The great advantage of depreciation is that it lets you reduce your taxes for as long as you own the asset. Keep in mind that when you sell the property, you may have to pay a depreciation recapture tax.

What is house hacking?

You may have heard people talk about hacking their way into the housing investment market or hacking their house. There are several versions of house hacking, and you can design your own. It's a way to start, in some cases. It can be renting out part of your home to pay the expenses (freeing up your income to use investing in more properties, perhaps) or living in one unit of a four-plex and renting out the other three.

Recently, house hacking has spilled over into the short-term rental market in some areas. A house hacker may use one of the popular online rental sites to rent out all or part of a residence to cover their home's carrying costs. This practice may be stepping over local renting regulations; so, check before you jump in.

Suppose you can qualify for a government-backed multi-family mortgage loan (like Fannie Mae or Freddie Mac). In that case, you can start off with a small multi-family dwelling complex for house hacking as your entry into rental property management with a low down payment requirement.

Chapter 8
Multi-family housing and commercial property

Multi-family housing

Housing with more than five dwelling units is considered multi-family, and this investment sector sits on the fence between residential and commercial property. There are small apartment complexes, garden units that are one or two stories surrounding courtyards or other amenities, mid-rise complexes that are larger and may have up to 9 levels, and high-rise apartments over 10 stories.

Some sources consider student and senior living facilities as part of the multi-family genre, while others include those specialties as part of the commercial sector. We will address those later. Other commercial sectors include office, retail, and industrial, with multiple subsectors in each.

In all of these, properties can be classified as A, B, or C.

In multi-family housing, referred to as MFH, Class A investments are luxury properties. They are high value complexes, offering more amenities, higher rents, and higher investments. Class B apartment complexes have good locations and good quality but not as many modern amenities as Class A. They may be slightly older. Class C properties are typically outdated and offer the lowest rent and lowest investment entry.

Across the U.S. the share of adults choosing (or needing) to rent instead of own has been slowly creeping up, and research suggests that millennials and Gen-Z are going to continue the trend. This fact is good news for MFH investors. Lenders are optimistic about the near-term prospects for opportunities in the multi-family arena.

Often, lenders find less risk in MFH loans compared to single-family rental mortgages, since the presence of multiple tenants diffuses the impact of a vacancy. If you have 20 units, losing one tenant is a much smaller hit to the cash flow than if you are renting out a single-family home or duplex. Another advantage to MFH is the short term of leases. Unlike the long-terms found in the office and retail sectors, apartment leases are typically one to two years. While this may increase turnover, it allows for quick response to changing market conditions and adjustments to rent as needed.

Depending on the size of the apartment complex, the use of a property management company now becomes much more likely, and your cash flow will be impacted as a result. But at the same time, your focus can shift to managing your investments rather than interacting with tenants and tenant issues.

Return on investment

The ROI, or return on investment, is a calculation of your property's profitability as a percentage of the cost. To determine the ROI for a cash purchase, you take the net profit and divide it by the purchase price. If you have a mortgage, you include the down payment, mortgage, and other impacts such as expenses in the calculation. Remember that we talked about using leverage in real estate investments. When you calculate the ROI for investment properties, the less cash you put into a real estate asset, the higher the ROI will be.

Commercial property

Typically, commercial property investments (retail, office, industrial, warehouse, and mixed use) have a higher potential return than single-family real estate. The ROI can be 6-12%, although the return is also more volatile and market specific. There are other advantages to commercial properties, as well, including these:

Pricing is more straightforward. Commercial property sales can be guided by income statements and other neutral, fact-based pieces of data.

Favorable lease terms. With many commercial properties, the owner can negotiate a triple net lease (sometimes called NNN). In such a case, the lessee pays virtually all of the expenses associated with operating the building, excluding the mortgage. High-quality, national chains often occupy their locations using this kind of lease, and these arrangements are frequently for extended terms. Because a major retailer does not want to change locations often, the owner enjoys stability, and the lessee typically takes excellent care of the property.

These NNN leases are available for the best properties, but even second tier assets have terms that are more favorable to the owner than residential rentals in many cases. Commercial tenants are accustomed to shouldering some of the expenses, and negotiation is flexible.

Business hours. In many commercial properties, unlike residential, the hours of operation are limited. Even in restaurant operations, most do not operate 24 hours a day. If your tenant does, you are still unlikely to be involved in the late-night concerns, as you will probably have a professional manager handling the property problems.

Sector volatility

On the other hand, investing in commercial property requires a higher initial investment and involves greater risk exposure. Probably no one predicted the hit that commercial real estate took in 2020 from the COVID-19 pandemic. There is no denying that individual sectors have been adversely impacted—commercial property transactions fell 57% year over year in the third quarter of 2020. Price increases in the apartment and industrial sectors outweighed declines in the retail and office sectors. Within retail, subsectors were unevenly tested. While grocery thrived, malls suffered. Strip malls and hospitality properties have been vulnerable, while warehouse and self-storage have benefitted.

Predictions for 2021 include lower transaction volume across the board but price improvements, particularly for life-science and data center properties, while retail and hotel values continue dropping.

Partnerships and LLCs

Suppose you want to invest in significant real estate assets with income potential but do not have access to the capital necessary to do so on your own. In that case, you can choose several options for involvement. The most straightforward approach is through a partnership or LLC with partners or investors. A partnership can be an LLC (limited liability corporation) or use a different structure, but the LLC is the most common for a small organization.

Business partners co-own a business and work together to achieve their goals. They may have similar or divergent skills and abilities. The partnership can be an even 50-50 split or some other division, as agreed in advance. If you have investors, they contribute money and receive a share of the profits but do not participate in decisions.

A general partnership is joint ownership of the business in which both parties have an equal right and shared liability.

A limited partnership has two categories of partners: general partners who share the business and the liability, and limited partners who invest in the business but do not share in decision-making and are not liable for the business's risks.

A limited liability partnership is a general partnership with some limited personal liability. This can be a sole proprietorship or a partnership. It can be used to limit personal liability.

Chapter 9

Fractional Investments

A highly popular investment method in large-scale income-producing commercial property is to buy shares in a **REIT** (real estate investment trust). Think of a REIT as the real estate equivalent of a mutual fund for stocks. In a mutual fund, suppose the fund owns 100 individual stocks. Each investor owns an equivalent share of those 100 stocks. In a REIT, the trust owns 100 properties; so, each investor in the trust owns an equal stake in those 100 properties.

REITs come in all shapes and sizes. They typically buy real estate properties, hold, operate, and manage them for profit. The REIT may focus on office property, warehouses, retail assets, hotels and other hospitality, housing, or other sectors. They may be in a particular geographic or economic niche or specialize in some other way.

Legally, a REIT must return at least 90% of its taxable income to the shareholders. It must also derive a minimum of 75% of the trust income from real estate activities and have 75% of the assets in real estate. A REIT must have at least 100 shareholders and cannot be majority owned by five or fewer people.

The reason this is true is in the origin of the REIT, which started in the Cigar Excise Tax Extension of 1960, passed by Congress and signed by then-President Eisenhower, who championed the concept. REITs can avoid paying corporate income tax on their profits to the extent that they share that income as dividends with their shareholders. Combined with the 90% distribution stipulation, this makes REITs a favorable channel for funneling profits into the wallets of shareholders.

Unlike owning a corporate stock, where the company must pay its tax obligations before sending profits to shareholders, the REIT shareholder will receive a distribution of income on which the REIT has not had to pay taxes. If the investor also holds the investment in a tax advantaged account (a 401(k) or IRA, for example), the tax benefit multiplies. If the investor maintains the REIT shares in a regular account, the REIT distribution is eligible for the deduction of up to 20% in the Tax Cut and Jobs Act of 2017 on pass-through income.

Some REITs are publicly traded, like stocks; others are not traded, although they register with the SEC; and still others are privately held. Each has different risks and benefits. Private REITs are usually only available to accredited investors, which means a person with gross income over $200,000 in each of the last two years (or joint income with a spouse above $300,000). Private REITs typically have a long initial holding term and can be hard to sell. Since they don't register with the SEC, they don't have to file any financial reports. For most people, these are not suitable investments.

The non-traded REIT is more difficult for a potential investor to research. You may not have access to adequate information to assess the goals and intentions of the REIT manager. You may not even be able to find out what assets the REIT is buying, holding, or selling.

The non-traded REIT may be complicated to sell quickly (illiquid investment). You may be obligated to hold the shares for a minimum time (often seven years), but buyers may be hard to find even if there is no required holding period. The absence of turnover does allow management to focus on a longer-term strategy, which can improve results.

Some non-traded REITs have high upfront fees and external managers, which can reduce the profits for investors. There are often concerns about the lack of transparency.

The publicly traded REIT is vulnerable in a rising interest rate environment when capital may go into bonds. These shares are more volatile than the non-traded or private REITs, potentially leaving the investor at the mercy of market drops. The upside of that is high liquidity and accessibility with no minimum investment amount.

Mortgage REITs

As mentioned, REITs own various property types. Any given trust could specialize by sector, price range, region, property age, lease type, or any combination of factors to create a focus that brings it the level of diversity or specificity the board of directors seeks.

Less common but also profitable are mortgage REITs. These are essentially finance companies that make loans collateralized by real estate but don't own assets. Sometimes called mREITs, these specialized trusts help support the U.S. housing market by providing liquidity through purchasing mortgage-backed securities. mREITs also work in the commercial market.

In general, buying shares of a REIT is a very attractive method of diversifying your real estate holdings, improving your geographic footprint, and expanding into classes and markets you might not otherwise be able to jump into on your own.

In the next section, we will investigate the tax deferral techniques you can use to retain the gains you earn on property investments and how to share wealth with your family, both now and after your death. At the beginning of the book we introduced the discussion of capital gains taxes and how the rate is lower than the rate on ordinary income, which is an advantage to investors. By using legal tax techniques such as a 1031 exchange, a Qualified Opportunity Zone, or a Delaware Statutory Trust, you can avoid paying even the capital gains tax rate on the money you earn by selling real estate. You can use these tools to continue investing in direct assets (owning property individually) or moving among fractional investments such as REITs.

Section 6
Maximizing Accumulation

Accumulating wealth through any legal means is a great goal. Maximizing the amount you keep, as opposed to what you share with the government in taxes, is a crucial component of the accumulation strategy. We have discussed in depth how the tax codes favor certain kinds of income over others, imposing lower tax rates on capital gains than ordinary income, as one example.

Remember that a capital gain is an increase in an asset's value that results in the asset having a higher worth than its basis. The basis is the cost of the asset (price plus acquisition expenses and improvements, if applicable) minus depreciation. If a property is held for less than one year, the gain is short-term and taxed at the taxpayer's ordinary income rate. If the investor owned the asset for more than one year, the growth is considered long-term, and the corresponding tax rate is lower.

As a reminder, consider this illustration:

You purchase a rental home and own it for 10 months. The purchase price, including acquisition costs, is $100,000. You sell it for $140,000, a gain of $40,000. Suppose you are in the 35% tax bracket. Your tax due on the gain from this sale is $14,000. With a tax rate of 35% on ordinary income, your capital gains rate will probably be 15%, although it might be 20%. In this scenario, a 15% bracket will result in a tax due of $6,000, while 20% will require $8,000. Both results are more attractive than paying $14,000 of your profit or gain as you would if you sold the property less than a year after the purchase.

CHAPTER 10

DEFERRING TAXES ON CAPITAL GAINS

Certainly, it's better to pay a lower tax rate than a higher one, but it's even better to keep the entire gain and continue investing the money to accumulate more money. You can legally do this in several ways.

1031 Exchange

The commonly referenced "1031 exchange," which is also often called a "like-kind" exchange, was not in the original Revenue Act of 1891, nor was any other tax deferral structure. The Revenue Act of 1921 added Section 202(c) to the Internal Revenue Code, which gave taxpayers the right to trade securities and non-like-kind properties if the property did not have a realizable market value. However, in 1935 the Board of Tax Appeals allowed an exchange that included cash, setting the stage for the 1954 renaming of the Section to 1031 by the 1954 Tax Code Amendments.

That Act defined the like-kind exchange provision. However, it was rarely used, since it literally required the two property owners to perform a simultaneous exchange of assets. Investor A would have to find Investor B, holding the exact property he wanted to acquire for the same value at the same time.

The nature of the 1031 exchange was dramatically altered by court cases involving the Starker family sale of timberland to Crown Zellerbach Corporation. Starker and Zellerbach's agreement called for a delayed deal and delayed compensation, which the IRS did not accept. Litigation between the Starkers, Zellerbach, and the IRS ultimately resulted in the establishment of the current practice of delayed exchanges with very strict and specific timelines for the identification and acquisition of replacement properties for qualification.

You can use a 1031 exchange over and over as long as you continue reinvesting the capital back into a new property. The exchange process is an excellent way to diversify your real estate portfolio, change your geographic concentration, or even transition from direct ownership to fractional, if that is a goal. **It's key to remember that a 1031 exchange is a deferral of capital gains tax, not an elimination.** Suppose you executed 10 simultaneous exchanges in a row, reinvesting the gains continually (not more than annually, of course) in like-kind properties. On the 11th transaction, you fail to qualify the exchange. You would then owe the taxes due not only on the last transaction but on the previous ones for which you were able to defer, as well. The only way to achieve a permanent deferral is to bequeath the final property. The heir receives a one-time step-up in basis that could eliminate those accumulated liabilities.

How does a 1031 exchange work?

Suppose you are the investor that wants to perform a 1031 exchange. You have a residential property, and you would prefer to have an office building, for example.

First, you need to engage a **qualified intermediary**. This person (or company) will manage the selling and buying transactions on your behalf and safeguard the proceeds during the interim period. This individual is crucial, because one of the requirements for a successful 1031 exchange is that the investor/taxpayer must not have access to the funds. The qualified intermediary (QI) is responsible for ensuring that the transactions are at arm's length and must receive the proper identification of replacement properties from the investor.

The IRS does not establish what qualifications the QI will have but does specify that the person cannot be any of the following:

⟩ Related to the investor (although a relationship as in-law is allowed, such as brother-in-law)

⟩ Married to the investor

⟩ An agent of the investor (this includes your attorney, accountant, real estate broker, and financial advisor)

⟩ Employed by the investor

Your financial advisor or accountant will probably be able to recommend a QI if you need one. While they are not required to be licensed or certified, an association called the Federation of Exchange Accommodators promotes high standards in the industry and offers continuing education for practitioners.

The IRS has been generally flexible in accepting the type of properties exchanged as "like-kind" as long as both the original (relinquished) and new (replacement) property are held for investment or business. You may not exchange a primary residence for a rental or an office building for a vacation home. Where there is strict adherence to the rules is in the timeline of identification and consummation.

1031 Exchange Timeline

Day 1: sale of original property

Day 45: formal identification of replacement property or properties

Day 180: completion of replacement purchase

The identification of replacement properties by the taxpayer is a formal process. The investor has three options for choosing how to select potential assets with which to replace the original (relinquished) property and **must present these to the QI within 45 days of the sale.** The options are:

Option 1: Identify no more than three properties as possible purchases. If you limit the number to three, there are no limits imposed on their individual or combined market price.

Option 2: Identify any number of replacement properties that all together do not exceed in value two times the price of the property sold. If the relinquished property is worth $2 million, the seller can identify replacement choices totaling up to $4 million.

Option 3: Identify any number of properties, but you must ultimately buy some subset with a value of at least 95% of the identified properties' combined value. For example, if you identify 10 replacement properties with total market value all combined of $20 million, you must purchase a subset of those properties with a purchase price of at least $19 million.

When executing any option, keep in mind that if the relinquished property's price is higher than the cost of the replacement property (or properties), the difference will be taxed as a capital gain. The full benefit of the exchange is in replacing the original property with one of equal or higher value to defer the recognition of the gain.

The other timeline element is the overall completion, which the investor must finish by day 180 of the original sale. If the exchange sale includes any improvements (building or repairs), those must be completed within that time, which is aggressive. This scenario has encouraged the growth of reverse exchanges, which are identical to traditional delayed exchanges but in reverse.

Reverse 1031 exchange

In a reverse 1031 exchange transaction, you as the investor might find a property you think is an ideal addition to your portfolio and decide to buy it. If so, you must complete the transaction through the use of a qualified intermediary, since that person must hold temporary title to the new property (and may be referred to as an exchange accommodation titleholder). The timeline goes in reverse, with 45 days available for you to determine the property that will be relinquished and 135 more to complete the exchange.

How critical is the QI role?

We can't exaggerate the importance of the qualified intermediary. That person (or entity, as the presence of QI firms becomes more common) is vital to the successful completion of the exchange and its allowance by the IRS. The QI must fulfill all these functions:

⟩ Coordinate with the seller and buyer(s) on the structure of the exchange

⟩ Prepare numerous documents regarding all assets involved

⟩ Maintain escrow accounts

⟩ Maintain arm's length in transactions to avoid the seller having constructive access to funds

⟩ Receive and acknowledge the formal replacement property identification

⟩ Complete the purchase of replacement property or properties in their name and later transfer to the investor

The intermediary may be affiliated with a title company, a legal partnership, or be a sole service provider. Many work on a fee-for-service basis. Some are also compensated by their access to interest accruing in the funds for which they have fiduciary responsibility. All agreements should be transparent. Consider that separate escrow accounts are safer than commingled funds.

Can I use a 1031 exchange to buy fractional property investments?

Yes. Investors can use an UPREIT (Umbrella Partnership Real Estate Investment Trust) or a DST (Delaware Statutory Trust) to transition from whole property ownership to fractional investments. There are numerous reasons to consider doing this:

Shifting from active to passive investment. Investors at some stage in their lives may decide they no longer want to be actively involved in real estate management. Fractional investment is an excellent option for those investors. The trust management owns and manages the property, while the investors have no control.

Diversifying. For investors who want to diversify, whether by sector or geography, fractional investments are a simple method of achieving the goal.

How do you invest in an UPREIT?

Strictly speaking, an UPREIT is more of a vehicle for investment than an actual investment type. It is a way to transfer a property from individual ownership into a trust in exchange for a stake in the trust. The owner of a property that has increased in value trades it to the

REIT (like a 1031 exchange) and receives operating partnership units in the REIT in return.

The investor does not have to convert the operating partnership units into REIT shares until they want to. If/when that conversion occurs and the investor sells the shares, the capital gain would be realized; so, this is the end of the line for 1031 deferrals. Using the UPREIT conversion is an excellent tool for estate planning, because the heir can convert the operating partnership units in REIT shares and benefit from the step-up in basis, avoiding capital gains on the original contributed property.

Is it a smart move?

Every investor must decide how much of their portfolio to hold in direct ownership and how much (if any) belongs in fractional investments. All investments have risks. Some REITs are traded publicly, and it is easier for investors to find information about those. Still, it may not be as easy to facilitate an UPREIT into a publicly traded trust. The REIT management may not be open to acceptance of an individual property. They may prefer the consistency of cash investments. There are privately traded REITs which may be more open to the concept, but those may be less liquid and harder to get good information about the performance.

As mentioned previously, a REIT must distribute at least 90% of the trust's taxable income every year to the shareholders. As a result, REITs are reliable sources of income for shareholders. UPREIT investors must meet the income requirements for accredited investors.

One risk to an investor entering into an UPREIT transaction is if the trustee decides to sell the property that the investor contributed. This situation is beyond the investor's control but would automatically result in the taxpayer having to recognize the taxable value gain. Other potential concerns include a merger or takeover of the REIT or a reduction in debt held that could impact the investor's operating partnership unit status. Frequently the original transaction between the contributor and the trust will address these potential minefields.

Can I 1031 exchange into and out of a DST?

Unlike the end of the line with an UPREIT, you can use a 1031 exchange to enter and exit a Delaware Statutory Trust. DSTs also offer income, similar to the distributions you may find in a successful REIT. A DST is also a passive real estate investment, usually diversified to some extent but often focused on a particular sector. For many investors, DST ownership provides the opportunity to invest in commercial properties that are larger and more valuable than those they could access independently.

Since a DST is treated as a security under U.S. law, it is the same as direct ownership of real estate for purposes of Section 1031 exchanges, and, therefore, eligible for a trade in and then out when the DST liquidates. The benefits of investing in a DST include:

⟩ Institutional grade assets
⟩ Professional management
⟩ Packaged offerings
⟩ Ease of completing the 1031 timely

- Exact size for the replacement value
- Diversification

There are risks or potential pitfalls to the DST investment (whether you enter it with a 1031 exchange or through a traditional purchase):

- Can't raise additional capital
- Investors have no control
- Long holding period requirements

Two particular advantages of DSTs are filling in the gaps of a 1031 exchange and generational planning. In the gap scenario, suppose you are engaged in a 1031 exchange. You sold the property you wanted to divest and identified some replacements that don't quite have the value you need to replace it. You can make an investment in a DST of the precise amount you need to achieve the number you are aiming for, and typically, you can easily do so within a 1031 timeline.

DSTs are also commonly viewed as an asset in the transition from active to passive management, which may be for generational planning or other reasons. Since DSTs are directly invested in property, an investor can use a DST investment as a means of exploring a sector in which they have no existing expertise if they trust the DST sponsor.

Qualified Opportunity Zones

Part of the Tax Cuts and Jobs Act of 2017 is the Investment in Opportunity Act, known as the Opportunity Zone Program. The goal is to direct capital gains into federally designated economically "challenged" areas called Qualified Opportunity Zones (QOZs).

Money invested into projects in such places, if the programs are designed to boost economic growth, can receive deferral from capital gains taxes.

The intent is not sufficient, however. The Act requires significant results, which is one of several reasons that QOZ investments are risky.

Under the program, the Treasury Department has named over 8,700 zones in the United States (and U.S. territories) in low-income areas. If you have a capital gain, you can defer the tax by reinvesting into a Qualified Opportunity Fund within 180 days of the gain. The investment guidelines allow three escalating benefits:

    I.   Deferral. If you direct assets with gains into a QOF, the gains will not be taxed until December 31, 2026, or until the asset is sold, whichever is first.

    II.   Step-up in basis. If you leave capital gains in a QOF for at least five years, you earn a step-up in the basis on the original investment of 10%. Leaving the money in the fund for seven years will result in a step-up of 15% over the initial investment. (Note that since the legislation benefit expires in 2026, this is not currently applicable unless the provisions are extended.)

    III.   Elimination. If you direct assets into a QOF for 10 years, you can exclude the capital gains from taxes permanently.

    IV.   In the last three-plus years, these QOZ investments have attracted over $75 billion. There are funds in real estate, alternative energy, professional services, start-ups in an array of businesses from tech to healthy food to cannabis delivery.

V. It's important to note that QOZ investments are high-risk and may not be suitable for everyone. Because the program is so new and may attract some very aggressive sponsors, some of the QOF managers are inexperienced. Some may not have a fully developed business plan appropriate to the location or environment. It may also be difficult for the potential investor to unearth adequate information about the track record of the partnerships and LLCs driving these funds. Be careful.

The family office and generational planning

A family office is a private wealth management operation that provides comprehensive financial and investment services to one or more extremely wealthy family units. The services will include financial advice, investment management, budgeting, accounting, insurance, philanthropic leadership, tax service and direction, and others as needed. A family office may also manage non-financial tasks, including travel, education, household management, and ancillary responsibilities. In some cases, ultra-high net worth individuals use a family office staff to manage their personal lives like the CEO's administrative assistant manages their work life. This support role can be even more critical after retirement but is still secondary to the other functions.

Chapter 11

Minimizing Capital Gains on Stocks

Previously we discussed the distinction between short- and long-term capital gains with stock investments—if you own a stock for less than a year, the gain when you sell it is taxed at the higher ordinary income rate. If you sell a stock investment you have held for more than a year, you pay taxes at the lower capital gain tax rate.

Remember, if you hold the stock in a tax advantaged account such as your 401(k) or IRA, those gains are not taxed. You will pay taxes later on the withdrawals from the account after retirement. The beauty of tax advantaged accounts is growing your earnings with no tax due.

Of course, there are limits to how much you can contribute to those accounts; so, you may own stocks in non-advantaged accounts, and hopefully, they are doing well. Paying taxes on the capital gain is something to celebrate, after all; it shows your investments are prospering. You also have the option to continue holding. You do not pay taxes on a gain you do not realize by selling the stock.

But if you sell, minimizing the tax you owe and pay is still a good goal. Let's look at some strategies to reduce the taxes owed on those gains.

Matching gains and losses

Sometimes you win; sometimes you lose. If you have stocks you have sold at a loss, those losses balance the gains and eliminate the need to pay taxes. If your net capital losses exceed your capital gains in a given year, you can actually use the capital loss to offset ordinary income, up to $3,000. Let's look at some examples:

Example A: You sell Stock X for a gain of $10,000 and Stock Y for a loss of $5,000. Subtract the loss from the gain (and here we are assuming that both have been held for over one year), and you pay capital gains tax on $5,000.

Example B: You sell stock X for a loss of $10,000 and Stock Y for a gain of $5,000, leaving you with an excess loss of $5,000. You pay no tax on Stock Y's growth and can use the remaining loss to offset ordinary income (from wages or salary). You still have $2,000 in losses you have not used to offset any gains (and can't use against ordinary income due to the limit). If you have no other capital gains to match, you can carry that remaining amount over to the following year and use it to offset further gains or ordinary income.

Tax loss harvesting

Tax loss harvesting is deciding to sell a stock which has lost value for the purpose of offsetting a gain on a well-performing stock. Suppose you have decided to sell Stock A, which has appreciated substantially. You want to offset the increase to minimize the tax you owe; so, you decide to sell Stock B, which has lost value. This action is a tax loss harvest and a legitimate strategy.

If you believe in the long-term value of Stock B, which may be suffering a temporary hardship, you can buy it again. Make sure you wait more than 30 days after the sale so you do not trigger a "wash sale" rule violation. The wash sale rule would disqualify the capital loss and also be activated if your spouse or a company you control bought the security.

Remember, when you re-purchase that stock, the clock resets on the one-year requirement for a long-term capital gain; so, you should not plan to use this strategy often.

Spread the gain (and the pain) out

Again, the catalyst for realizing the tax owed is the sale, not the appreciation in value. If you own a stock that is going "through the roof" and you just watch it go, there is no tax consequence. The tax obligation comes when you decide to sell it. If you are selling for portfolio balance or to fund a purchase, you may be able to control the timing. One practice is to split the sales over two or even three tax years. Here is an example:

You want to sell 100,000 shares of Stock C, which has increased in value during the five years you owned it. You stagger the sales so that your gains are separated into three different years, and you can either offset with losses or at least spread out the obligation.

Give stock instead of cash

Giving stock to charity and your heirs can be an advantage to you and them. If you have favorite nonprofit organizations, consider making gifts in appreciated stock rather than cash. You should be able to claim a deduction for the current fair market value of the security (assuming you have held it for more than a year, as usual). You can use the cash you would have contributed for the investment you want to make. Here is an example:

You plan to contribute $20,000 to Charity X, your alma mater. You would receive a deduction of $20,000. You also want to sell $20,000 of Stock G you bought five years ago for $10,000, which is a gain of $10,000. Assuming you are paying a capital gains tax rate of 15%, you will owe $1,500 on the income. If, instead, you are paying the higher 20% rate, your tax due is $2,000.

If you instead contribute the $20,000 of Stock G to Charity X, you will pay no capital gains tax, and you get a deduction for $20,000, the fair market value of the stock. Your alma mater has received the same value, and you can invest the cash into new investments (or whatever other purpose you intend).

Bequeathing stock to your heirs has the same result if you give the security rather than the proceeds. The heirs receive a step-up to market value at the time of your death; so, no one pays capital gains tax on the appreciated value.

Chapter 12

Estate Planning

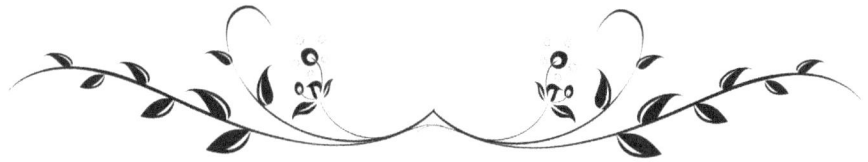

Wills and Trusts

Wills and trusts are tools that help with your assets' disposition after your death and can help protect those assets as they pass to your heirs. If you are married, the United States Estate and Gift Tax law allows for an unlimited transfer of wealth to the surviving spouse without any gift or estate tax liability.

A will is an expression of the writer's wishes and takes effect when the writer dies. In addition to the transfer of property and money, a will is typically used for granting guardianship of minor children. Trusts dispense assets either before or after death. Some are revocable, and others are not. Wills must proceed through the probate process, which is an examination by a court administrator, while trusts usually do not.

Living trust

Living revocable trusts are common and generally established for the purpose of transferring property to heirs. They are set up while the grantor is still living, and because they are revocable, the grantor can change them, like a will, at any time. The property in the trust still belongs to the grantor as long as that person is living. There are also irrevocable trusts, which can't be altered once signed.

If the taxpayer is unmarried, a living trust may save money in comparison to a will by avoiding probate expenses. On the other hand, the trust will cost more to set up initially. If privacy is a concern, the trust is a better option, because wills are public records, while trusts are not.

A trust can be helpful in the event that you become unable to continue managing your financial and personal affairs, and the trustee can take over. However, this can become a point of contention if the trustee asserts that you are unable while you dispute the assertion.

Irrevocable trusts

Irrevocable trusts are not recommended for most investors. The three reasons to consider setting one up are:

   I. Reducing estate taxes. The estate must be huge to be subject to estate taxes, since the 2021 exemption is $11.7 million. This is not a widespread situation.
   II. Eligibility for disability benefits. Suppose you anticipate you may need to rely on programs like Medicaid and

Supplemental Security Income. In that case, you may want to consult an advisor about an irrevocable trust for your assets so you can maintain your eligibility. Again, the majority of high-wealth individuals are not going to be relying on these programs.

III. Protecting assets from lawsuits. An irrevocable trust can protect assets (if created in one of a handful of friendly states) from creditors. The grantors of these asset protection trusts are typically those professionals who frequently face extremely high-dollar lawsuits (obstetricians and other specialty medical professionals, some attorneys, and others).

There are downsides to tying up your assets in an irrevocable trust that are unlikely to be outweighed by the potential benefits. They are typically more expensive to set up and administer and can receive more onerous tax treatment. But most important, irrevocable means irrevocable.

If you have an irreconcilable conflict with someone to whom you have granted significant assets, you can't revoke the grant. You might have a genuinely worthy cause for disinheriting someone, but you can't.

If you want to sell property in the trust, you need permission to do so. Many things can change in your life, in the investment world, or the lives of the people involved in the trust (including the person selected as trustee) but irrevocable is permanent. Be very sure that's the right way to go before committing.

Inheritance

Renowned German literary figure and statesman Jonathan Goethe said, "What you inherit from your fathers, earn over again for yourselves, or it will not be yours."

Extremely wealthy American industrialist Andrew Carnegie did not believe in bequeathing wealth to his children (or even his wife). He said, "I would as soon leave my son a curse as the almighty dollar." His will distributed his vast assets to a variety of philanthropic organizations.

For most people, the dream of leaving an inheritance to their children is an ardent goal, the culmination of a life's work. If you have accumulated wealth in real estate or stocks, the measures we have recommended to defer recognition of capital gains taxes on the appreciation will pay off when you give those assets to your heirs.

For both stocks and property, the heir will receive a step-up in the tax basis when they receive the asset due to inheritance. Let's look at examples for clarification.

Suppose you own rental properties. If you purchased a single-family residence for $100,000 and held onto it for 20 years, it might be worth $500,000. If you sell that property, you will pay taxes on the gain of $400,000 (subject to the mitigating strategies and other measures we have discussed). If you direct that property to your heir, the heir receives a step-up in basis to the fair market value at the time of your death; so, the heir's basis is now $500,000. If they sell it, they will not owe a tax, because there is no capital gain.

The same applies to stock. If you hold a stock for some time and it appreciates in value, you do not owe taxes on the increase if you do not sell it. Instead, in your will or trust, you direct it to your heir. When you die, the heir benefits from the step-up in value to the current fair market price and can hold it or sell without owing a capital gain tax.

You can pass along assets with total value and no tax consequences. If you need to sell before transferring the investment, you should look for one of the deferral means we have discussed.

These methods of accumulating wealth and reducing the amounts you pay in taxes are suggested as general strategies. Every taxpayer and investor should proceed according to their own circumstances. Earlier we discussed risk tolerance and risk capacity. These are key to successful and satisfactory investing. No one should risk money they can't afford to lose. Planning for the future is important, as is enjoying the present day.

This final quote is attributed to St. Luke. "Remember the past, plan for the future, but live for today, because yesterday is gone and tomorrow may never come."

www.ingramcontent.com/pod-product-compliance
Lightning Source LLC
Chambersburg PA
CBHW050003230526
45465CB00003BB/1239